Poetry with a Purpose

Develop Reading Comprehension and Enrich Vocabulary

Verses by Ernestine Cobern Beyer

Edited by
Frances Fisher Allen and Barbara Beyer Malley

Illustrated by Grace Lawrence

Cover by Kathryn Hyndman

Copyright © Good Apple, Inc., 1987

ISBN No. 0-86653-415-6

Printing No. 987

GOOD APPLE, INC.
BOX, 299
CARTHAGE, IL 62321-0299

Contents

Preface

Early Contact with Poetry

In its infinite versatility, poetry has something for all of us. The themes are endless: animals, nature, people, fantasy, philosophy, social issues. Through poetry we see our own experiences reflected, or empathize with the experiences and feelings of others. We become more sensitive to what is going on around us, seeing new significance in everyday occurrences. Poetry can entertain us, calm us, arouse our passions, tingle our spines. Poetry satisfies a deep and ancient need.

Children's early contact with poetry begins with discussions about words and their connections with daily events. As they grow older, they become attuned to the subtleties, double meanings, and symbolism found in poetry.

As children awaken to poetry, teachers should look for these interconnected reactions: enjoyment, a desire for further exploration, and increased sensitivity to their mental and physical environments.

Children can be taught to explore and use an anthology for practical as well as aesthetic purposes. They enjoy hunting for an appropriate verse for an upcoming holiday or a relative's birthday. As they browse through anthologies, they become aware of poetry's diversity and scope. Their interest kindled, they are motivated to pursue and unearth finds of their own.

Children take particular delight in witty poems. Well-written humorous verse not only amuses them but also acquaints them with satire, irony, and innuendo. Their taste and discrimination will improve if they are continually exposed to good poetry. When introducing poetry to your class, try the following guidelines—they work!

Have readily accessible tapes and recordings of poems.

Have poetry anthologies on your bookshelf.

Read poetry aloud frequently.

Have choral readings—children love to participate in such activities.

Draw on the work of contemporary poets as well as time-tested selections.

Be sure the poems you select are comprehensible to children.

Be aware of children's attraction to poems with action and humor.

Let the class choose a weekly favorite for the bulletin board.

Encourage the writing of poetry.

Suggest that children draw pictures to illustrate their own visual poems; or use the poem itself to make a picture, as with this version of "Grapefruit" by Ernestine Cobern Beyer.

When I sit down at half-past eight
To eat the grapefruit on my plate,
"I hope," I say as juices fly,
"There's more to this
than meets the . . . ."

Writing Poetry

As a start, children can learn quite easily how to express their thoughts in haiku poems. A verse form invented by the Japanese, the haiku is composed of three lines with a total of 17 syllables: five/seven/five. Its theme is usually connected in some way with nature and is concerned with the present moment and the emotion of that moment. It must have a single effect, presenting only one idea, feeling, or image.

Although haiku are generally unrhymed, rhyme should not be precluded if it occurs naturally, without forcing. Ideas for haiku may be found everywhere. Children who master this skill will gain the confidence and self-discipline to try more elaborate constructions, such as the five-line cinquain with syllables measured two/four/six/eight/two. "Triad,"* by Adelaide Crapsey, is a classic example of this form:

> These be
> Three silent things:
> The falling snow . . . the hour
> Before the dawn . . . the mouth of one
> Just dead.

According to Riley Hughes, author of *How to Write Creatively*, "Being a creative person means being in touch with your uniqueness and sharing that uniqueness with others. Through your efforts to write creatively, through your attempts to become familiar with words and stay attuned to living language, you can become that creative person."

Poets aim to strip away the familiar, predictable meanings of objects and events in order to reveal their personal ideas. Most of us, if we see a weather vane, may notice its shape and perhaps the direction of the wind, but otherwise give it little thought. Ernestine Cobern Beyer, author of the verses in this book (except where otherwise noted), saw a weather vane and captured what it meant to her in the following lines:

The Weather Vane Horse

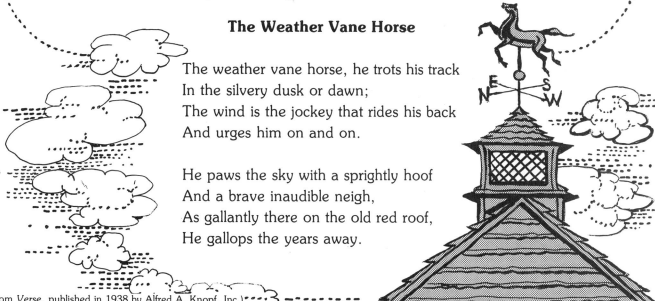

> The weather vane horse, he trots his track
> In the silvery dusk or dawn;
> The wind is the jockey that rides his back
> And urges him on and on.
>
> He paws the sky with a sprightly hoof
> And a brave inaudible neigh,
> As gallantly there on the old red roof,
> He gallops the years away.

*(from *Verse*, published in 1938 by Alfred A. Knopf, Inc.)

We take delight in children because they see the world with clear-eyed wonder. Their impressions are unsullied by past experiences, prejudices, or preconceived ideas as to how they should react. Poets, too, look with wonder at everyday objects; then with their unique perception they transform the ordinary into the beautiful. Something as prosaic as a grandfather clock was endowed by Ernestine Beyer with human sensibilities and an aura of mystery. To thus attribute human qualities to objects is a figure of speech called **personification**.

The Grandfather Clock

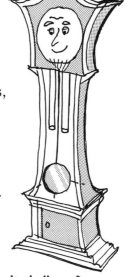

The grandfather clock on the stair,
How solemn and courtly his air!
With motionless hands he patiently stands,
Recalling a day more fair.

Never again will he start.
Silent, he stands there, apart,
Holding the hour when life was in flower
Forever unspent in his heart.

The poet personified a crocus in a poem called "David and Goliath."

Challenging his frosty foe
A crocus swaggers from the snow,
And with his tiny golden arrow
Pierces Winter to the marrow!

C. S. Lewis, author of novels about life on other planets, once said he wished animals could write books so he could see what the world was like from their perspective. A poet, though unable to **become** a hummingbird or a bee, is quite capable of imagining life on a tiny creature's level. Ernestine Beyer's "The Tippler" is a whimsical example of this art.

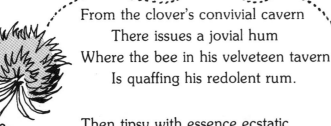

From the clover's convivial cavern
    There issues a jovial hum
Where the bee in his velveteen tavern
    Is quaffing his redolent rum.

Then tipsy with essence ecstatic
    Distilled in the summery dawn,
Off on an errand erratic
    He reels to his wings and is gone!

A successful poet is never casual with language but values each word and uses it with exquisite precision. Mark Twain observed that the difference between the right word and the almost-right word was the difference between lightning and a lightning bug. Note that the adjectives and verbs in "The Tippler" are not merely suitable or appropriate—they are so **right** that they strike the reader as inevitable. It would seem they were simply waiting for the author to give them life.

It is this love affair with words that marks the creative writer. Riley Hughes, in *How to Write Creatively*, observes that "poetry is the deep well from which words in their fullness of meaning may be drawn . . . . Words are alive in the dictionary, alive and waiting."

Our poet saw words as seeds in the following poem:

Seeds

The milkweed seeds drift lightly everywhere.
Carrying the weight of unborn springs,
They float along;
So seeds of thought that pollinate the air
Drift softly to my heart on filmy wings
To make a song.

Painters and poets use different tools but have a common objective: communication. A poet's raw materials are the words absorbed daily with a sensitized awareness of their sounds and meanings. A sure sign of a writer's skill with words is the ability to paint vivid verbal pictures—indeed, it often happens that the reader not only **sees** what is presented, but hears, smells, tastes, and feels it as well. In "The Troubadour," another poem celebrating the bee, Ernestine Beyer evokes four of our five senses with a few concise lines.

The bee's the minstrel of the air.
He is welcomed everywhere.
When they hear his mandolin,
Eager blossoms let him in.

Clad in brown and yellow bands,
Swaggering he lightly stands
On a carpet of perfume,
Strumming to a lily-bloom.

The term for poetic word pictures is **imagery**, another figure of speech like **personification**. In "The Firefly," our poet imagines that the insect uses a tiny flashlight to illuminate his world.

The Firefly

A firefly that tours my lawn
Turns his tiny flashlight on;
And with this valiant little spark
He bravely travels through the dark.

All night long he cruises there
On his avenue of air,
But daylight dims his winsome wink.
He has blown a fuse, I think!

Other charming word pictures are sketched in the following:

Goldfish

A wriggling comma, golden, small,
Tail tipped with lapis lazuli,
He slowly tours his glassy ball
Exhaling opals casually.

The Snail

Adventuring a tangled trail,
How slowly crawls the patient snail!
He pauses for a moment, brief,
To take the measure of a leaf;
Then up a twig and down a rose
His tiny covered wagon goes!

In *The Poet's Eye*, Arthur Alexander likens poetry to music: both have rhythm and concern for sound.

"Rhythm is the pulse of life in poetry. It helps to create the emotion we feel when we hear or read a poem . . . . We use the word *meter* to mean the measured rhythm a poet uses in his verse. Meter acts as a framework or skeleton and supports the poem."

The need for poetry has been with us from our very beginnings. Before the days of written language, people had to depend on oral tradition. The strolling minstrels and singing chroniclers, as purveryors of news and information, were aware that their listeners would longer remember songs and "newscasts" with regular rhythms.

A measured beat is one of poetry's greatest pleasures. "Perhaps we might say that poetry's metrical rhythm echoes something deep within man as important as the breath of life or the beat of a heart."

Alexander notes that a poem can have a perfect pattern, but it is nothing if it does not move us in some way. Poetry is one of the best ways to communicate the feelings and personal philosophy of a writer. Ernestine Beyer's mystical bent is evident in a poem called "Flight."

Flight

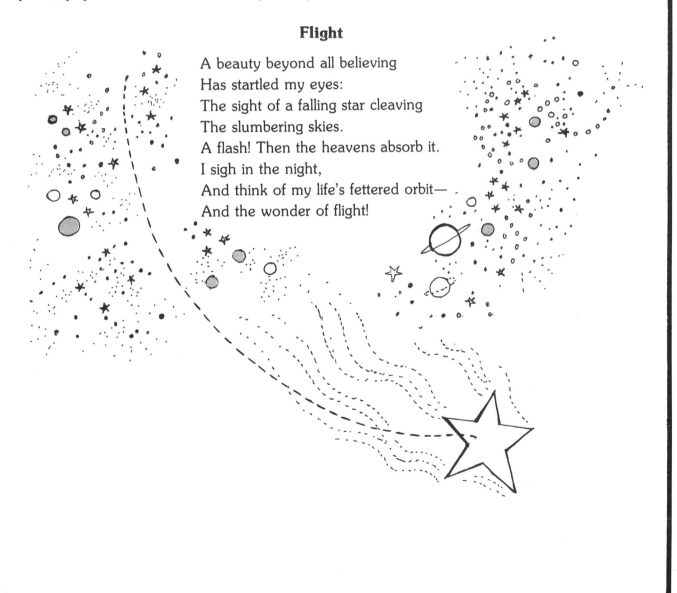

A beauty beyond all believing
Has startled my eyes:
The sight of a falling star cleaving
The slumbering skies.
A flash! Then the heavens absorb it.
I sigh in the night,
And think of my life's fettered orbit—
And the wonder of flight!

Elements of Poetic Style

Instinctively or deliberately, poets enhance the words they choose by arranging them alliteratively. **Alliteration** repeats the same letter at the beginning of two or more words in a line of poetry, creating a melodious effect. We have already seen plentiful examples of this language enhancer. In "The Tippler" alone, alliteration is used five times: "clover's convivial cavern," "redolent rum," "essence ecstatic," "distilled in the summery dawn," and "errand erratic."

In addition to figures of speech like **personification** and **imagery**, poets utilize **onomatopoeia**, words whose sounds imitate the objects or actions to which they refer. In "Sudden Silver," the word "corroborates" echoes the rumble of thunder. ("Rumble" is itself an onomatopoeic word.)

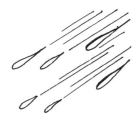

The air is chill. The clouds are rent asunder.
Upon the sky the lightning scribbles "Rain!"
"Rain!" corroborates the distant thunder,
And sudden silver glistens in the lane.

Sibilance, the use of words characterized by the sound of **s** or **z**, is also manifest in the above poem. The repeated hissing sounds are suggestive of falling rain.

Other figures of speech are the **similes** and **metaphors** which illuminate a poet's writing. A **simile** is a figure of speech in which two unlike things are compared, usually connected by the words "like" or "as." A **metaphor** transfers more directly the likeness or analogy between objects or ideas. "The lightning scribbles 'Rain!'" is a **metaphor**. In a **simile**, the poet would say "lightning is like scribbling in the sky." Almost every poem we have quoted contains fresh and sparkling **metaphors**. In "Seeds" the poet's **simile** likens seeds of thought to milkweed seeds.

A poet sometimes makes an exaggerated statement for literary effect, using a figure of speech called **hyperbole**. In "Birthington's Washday," which you will soon read, Ernestine Beyer's humorous use of **hyperbole** convinces us that Bertie is long overdue for a bath.

This book is intended primarily for vocabulary enrichment through the exploration of poetry. Children are fascinated with words and language; their minds can be trained to assimilate the rich and varied vocabulary found in poetry. This learning experience can be exciting for teachers and children alike.

We can give no better advice to students than that suggested by Arthur Alexander. "To understand what a poem is, read good poetry and try to write poetry yourself." He urges children to write poems whenever they feel like it. "No subject is unsuitable as long as you remember to be **personal** or be yourself when you write a poem."

In a final cautionary note, Alexander hopes we will not take poetry so seriously that its enjoyment is destroyed. It is in this spirit that the editors of this book invite you to turn to the first poem. Learn new words, value new words, but above all, have fun!

Birthington's Washday

Birthington Biddle (his friends called him Bertie)
Would have been nice if he hadn't been dirty.
So grubby and grimy was Birthington's face,
His appearance, alas, was a perfect disgrace.
You see, he believed soap and water were poison,
And tubs were for **clothes**—not to wash little boys in.
Crusted with dust which flew up from the street,
He grew heavier, daily, and slower of feet.
And though his poor mother could hardly endure him,
She couldn't, it seemed, either change him or cure him.

On the day he turned ten, Bertie found to his shame,
He could no longer run or take part in a game.
Just one final cinder, just one speck of dust
Had at last overburdened the weight of his crust.
Yes sir, one speck had stopped Bert in his track
Just as one final straw broke the poor camel's back.
Unable to move, Bertie let out a yelp . . .
A mud-smothered holler: "Help, Mother, help, help!"

Mrs. Biddle came running, and seizing a hose,
She hastily soused him from cowlick to toes.
The water gushed out in a glorious squirt,
And merrily melted his coating of dirt.
Thank goodness, that crust which had made him look fat
Was banished forever in two minutes flat!

His mother was filled with unspeakable joy
As she gazed at her clean little, **lean** little boy.
This was a day she would never forget—
His birthday! The day Dirty Bertie got wet!
That gurgle-and-slosh day, that sputter-and-splosh day,
Known in the village as Birthington's Washday!

Key Words

cowlick (kou´ lĭk) n. a tuft of hair that cannot be easily combed flat
Except for his **cowlick**, the boy's hair looked neatly combed.

cinder (sĭn´ dər) n. partly burned piece of coal or wood
The **cinder** from the fireplace fell onto the rug.

crust (krŭst) v. to form or harden into a crust or coating
The clam digger's hands were **crusted** with mud.

disgrace (dĭs grās´) n. shame
John's lack of respect for his parents was a **disgrace**.

endure (ĕn dŏŏr´) v. to hold up under pain or misfortune
I can't **endure** standing in line for an hour.

gaze (gāz) v. to look steadily
The teacher **gazed** at her students for a moment to gain their attention.

glorious (glôr´ ē əs) adj. magnificent; splendid
It was a **glorious** day—perfect for a picnic.

grimy (grī´ mē) adj. very dirty; covered with soot
The chimney sweep was **grimy** from head to foot.

grubby (grŭb´ ē) adj. dirty
After making mud pies, the little girls looked **grubby** but happy.

gurgle (gûr´ gl) v. to flow with a bubbling or gurgling sound
At night we can hear the trees whispering and the brook **gurgling**.

lean (lēn) adj. thin; not plump or fat
The forest ranger was a tall, **lean** man who had spent most of his life outdoors.

overburden (ō′vər bûr′dn) v. to weigh down; overload
The mule was **overburdened**, so he sat down and wouldn't move.

seize (sēz) v. to grasp suddenly
The pirates **seized** the gold from the ship.

slosh (slŏsh) v. to splash or move clumsily through water
As she **sloshed** through the puddles, she was glad she was wearing boots.

smother (smŭth′ər) v. to be without sufficient air; suffocate
She thought she would **smother** because of the thick smoke in the room.

souse (sous) v. to make soaking wet
He **soused** the lawn with the garden hose.

sputter (spŭt′ər) v. to speak explosively and incoherently
Upset over his dented fender, the man **sputtered** angrily that the collison wasn't his fault.

squirt (skwûrt) v. to shoot out in a thin stream
The boys **squirted** each other with the hose for fun.

unspeakable (ŭn spē′kə bəl) adj. inexpressible; indescribable; awesome
When the fireman rescued her baby, the mother's joy was **unspeakable**.

Comprehension Check

Check the answer.

1. Bertie believed soap and water were

    ____ a. fun to play in
    ____ b. poison
    ____ c. for grown-ups

2. Bertie wanted to

    ____ a. go swimming
    ____ b. take a bath
    ____ c. stay dirty

Fill in the blanks in the paragraph with the following words:

    a hose   move   dirt   help

Bertie couldn't _____ because he was covered with _____. His mother ran
                    (3)   (4)

to _____ him. She soused him with _____.
        (5)   (6)

7. Bertie was finally stopped in his track by

    ____ a. a large train
    ____ b. one tiny cinder
    ____ c. a policeman
    ____ d. his mother

8. Bertie's mother was unhappy because

    ____ a. Bertie played too much
    ____ b. Bertie took too many baths
    ____ c. Bertie talked back to her
    ____ d. Bertie was dirty

9. The lesson Bertie learned was that

    ____ a. it pays to be dirty
    ____ b. mother knows best
    ____ c. cleanliness is important
    ____ d. birthdays are important

10. This poem is mainly about
    ____ a. George Washington
    ____ b. Bertie's mother
    ____ c. a little boy who didn't like to bathe
    ____ d. games boys play

Think about: Do you think this was a true happening? Why?

The Concert

Yelchior, dressed in his black and his white,
Sat down on his skinny old shanks
And sang, the old dear, without worry or fear—
And, too, I might add, without thanks.

Outlined on the rail by a bleary-eyed moon,
He sang to a distant Maltese;
Keeping time with his tail, he emitted a wail
In eleven malevolent keys.

When windows flew open and nightcaps leaned out,
He was thrilled to his flattered old roots,
And he took a deep bow when his mounting me-ow
Brought a thundering salvo of boots.

"They cannot but recognize genius like mine!"
Thought Yelchior, dodging a shoe;
"Since they all stay awake for my talented sake,
I will now rend an encore or two!"

All evening he sang, but as dawn staggered in,
(Worn out by the concert, I guess),
He finished content, and he thought as he went:
"I am surely a howling success!"

Key Words

concert (kŏn′sûrt) n. a musical performance
The Rolling Stones gave a **concert** at Boston Garden.

content (kən tĕnt′) adj. happy enough with what one has or is
He was **content** with his home and his family.

dodge (dŏj) v. to move or twist suddenly, as to avoid a blow
We stopped to watch a boy **dodging** balls shooting out of a machine.

emit (ĭ mĭt′) v. to send out; utter
The cat **emitted** a horrible wail when its tail was stepped on.

encore (än′kōr) n. a repetition of a performance in answer to continued applause
The audience kept applauding until the performer sang several **encores**.

flatter (flăt′ər) v. to praise too much
Mrs. Smith was **flattered** by the young man's constant attention.

genius (jēn′yəs) n. a great mental and creative power
The **genius** graduated from Harvard when he was fifteen.

malevolent (mə lĕv′ə lənt) adj. wishing to harm others; malicious
With a **malevolent** smile, the boy broke the little girl's new toy.

Maltese (mŏl tēz′) n. a variety of domestic cat with bluish gray fur
A painting of a **Maltese** cat hung over the fireplace.

nightcap (nīt′kăp′) n. a cap worn in bed
The old lady was wearing a **nightcap** trimmed with lace.

rail (rāl) n. a horizontal bar of wood between upright posts
The cat was sitting on the **rail** of the fence.

recognize (rĕk′əg nīz) v. to approve of or appreciate
All of the students **recognized** their art teacher's talent.

rend (rĕnd) v. to tear apart; rip with violence
The roar of the jet **rends** the air.

salvo (săl′vō) n. a discharge of a number of firearms
A **salvo** of guns started the naval battle.

thundering (thŭn′dər ĭng) adj. thumping; whopping
The building crashed with a **thundering** noise that hurt my ears.

Comprehension Check

Check the answer.

1. Yelchior was a cat who

　　____a. was brown and white
　　____b. liked to chase squirrels
　　____c. thought he had a beautiful voice

2. Windows flew open because

　　____a. people liked to hear Yelchior sing
　　____b. people were throwing shoes at Yelchior
　　____c. people wanted to air out their houses

3. Yelchior thought he

　　____a. had nine lives
　　____b. knew how to dodge shoes
　　____c. was a howling success

Fill in the blanks in the paragraph with the following words:

　　　thanks　　　awake　　　yowling　　　shoes　　　concert　　　cat

Yelchior was a black and white _____. When he gave a_____, he didn't
　　　　　　　　　　　　　　　　　(4)　　　　　　　　　　　　　　　　(5)
get any _____. People threw _____ at Yelchior because he kept them
　　　　　　(6)　　　　　　　　　　　　(7)
_____ with his _____.
　　(8)　　　　　　　　　　(9)

10. This poem is mainly about

　　____a. a cat's midnight concert
　　____b. people who throw shoes
　　____c. how cats see in the dark

Think about: How would you solve the problem of cats yowling at midnight in your backyard?

_____

_____

_____

_____

The Donkey and the Cricket

A donkey, roly-poly, ambling lazily and slowly
By a tuneful little spoonful of a brook,
Heard a song as sweet as syrup. Charmed, the donkey pricked his ear up
With a listening, appreciative look.

As he spied the little cricket who was singing in the thicket,
"Bravo, bravo!" he exclaimed and made a bow.
"I hope you will not scruple to accept me as a pupil!
I have always yearned to sing. Pray teach me how!"

Said the cricket to the donkey: "There's a right key and a wrong key.
It's my **diet**, sir, that keeps my voice in tune,
So if you would be a singer you will be a real humdinger
If you dine on dewdrops mellowed by the moon!"

The donkey tried to do so. Did he sing, then, like Caruso?
Heavens no! His song became a bray at once.
He went back to eating clover, saying over, dear, and over:
"He who imitates another is a dunce."

11

Key Words

amble (ăm' bəl) v. to move with a leisurely gait; walk slowly
The two women **ambled** down the street, stopping now and then to look in shop windows.

appreciative (ə prē'shə tĭv) adj. approving; grateful
The girl was most **appreciative** of all the cards and letters she received during her illness.

bray (brā) v. to utter a loud, harsh cry
Foolish Pinocchio grew long ears and **brayed** like a donkey.

Caruso (kə rōō'sō) 1873-1921 Italian opera singer
Enrico **Caruso** is still remembered for his beautiful tenor voice.

humdinger (hŭm' dǐng' ər) n. something extraordinary; a marvel
The magician ended his act with a **humdinger** of a trick.

imitate (ĭm' ə tāt) v. to model oneself after the behavior of; copy
The baby tried to **imitate** the way his father was coughing.

mellow (mĕl'ō) v. to bring to maturity; ripen
Fruits are sweetest when they have **mellowed** on the vine.

pray (prā) v. to ask imploringly; beseech
"**Pray** tell, why do you look so sad?" the old woman asked her granddaughter.

roly-poly (rō'le-pō'lē) adj. short and plump
It was hard to believe this tall, slim young woman had been a **roly-poly** little girl.

scruple (skroo′pəl) v. to hesitate out of conscience or principle
The king didn't **scruple** to add to his riches by taxing the poor.

spy (spī) v. to catch sight of
As I hurried into the theatre, I **spied** a friend who was saving a seat for me.

tuneful (toon′fəl) adj. melodious; musical
During dinner, a musician played **tuneful** melodies on his accordion.

yearn (yûrn) v. to have a strong desire
The old man **yearned** to see his native land once more.

This is your space. You may:
    a. draw a picture about the poem
    b. write a story
    c. write a poem
    d. write a paragraph
Use at least three key words for b, c, or d.

Comprehension Check

Check the answer.

1. The donkey was

   ____a. as slim as a racehorse
   ____b. as big as an elephant
   ____c. roly-poly

2. The donkey wanted to be

   ____a. a violinist
   ____b. an orchestra leader
   ____c. a singer

Fill in the blanks in the paragraph with the following words:

diet   syrup   cricket   dewdrops   moon

The donkey heard a song as sweet as _____. He wanted the _____ to
                                        (3)   (4)

teach him how to sing. The cricket was able to sing beautifully because of his _____.
                                                                                   (5)

He dined on _____ mellowed by the _____.
                (6)   (7)

8. From this poem we learn

   ____a. how donkeys learn to sing
   ____b. what crickets eat
   ____c. it is wise to be yourself

9. It is clear that

   ____a. the donkey's bray is not melodious
   ____b. donkeys and crickets are friends
   ____c. crickets are good teachers

10. This poem is mainly about

    ____a. singing lessons
    ____b. how donkeys and crickets relate to each other
    ____c. differing capabilities

Think about: How would you teach your friend to play soccer?

_____

_____

_____

_____

The Lovable Dragon

Wilbur, the Lovable Dragon was hurt—
And with very good reason, I'm sad to assert.
Like all proper dragons, smoke, orange and red,
Poured from his nostrils and circled his head.
He **looked** so ferocious that children in fright
Took to their heels in unflattering flight.

One day he was stoking his personal stove
By eating red peppers that grew in a grove
When along came Chief Thundercloud's prettiest daughter,
Known in the village as Little Bright Water.
She carried a handful of corn as she came
To throw at the birds that were hungry and tame.
She came upon Wilbur, who, much to her panic,
Behaved with a warmth that was almost volcanic.
Puffing and snorting, he blithely came up
And frolicked around like a lovable pup.
Too frightened to speak, she couldn't have fled—
But in terror, she hurled all her corn at his head.
It flew all about him. Then, harmlessly dropping,
The corn she had thrown began merrily popping!
That funny hot snow—oh, it smelled very good!
Should she sample a flake? . . . She decided she would.

Wilbur, the Lovable Dragon, my dear,
Thereafter was happy for many a year.
Children adored him! And grateful and lovin',
They fed him red peppers to heat up his oven.
Famous was Wilbur, and very contented . . .
And that is how popcorn, I think, was invented!

15

Key Words

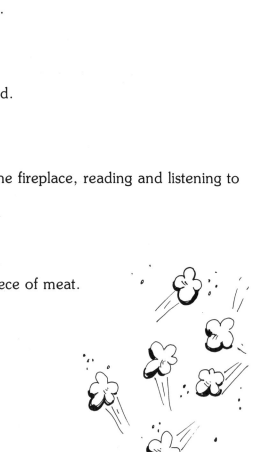

adore (ə dōr) v. to love; idolize
The girls had always **adored** their grandmother.

assert (ə sûrt) v. to declare; say
I heard him **assert** that he had been at the meeting.

behave (bē hāv) v. to act; conduct oneself
The baby **behaved** beautifully on the bus trip to Canada.

blithely (blīth´ lē) adv. cheerfully; lightheartedly
The little girl was **blithely** playing hopscotch with a friend.

contented (kən tĕn´ tĭd) adj. pleased; satisfied
On cold days, the old couple was **contented** to sit by the fireplace, reading and listening to music.

ferocious (fə rō´shəs) adj. fierce
The **ferocious** lions were fighting and snarling over a piece of meat.

flee (flē) v. to run away
The kitten **fled** when she saw the puppy.

frolic (frŏl´ ĭk) v. to act playful
The two colts **frolicked** in the meadow.

grateful (grāt´ fəl) adj. thankful
We were **grateful** for the fine sailing weather during our vacation.

grove (grōv) n. a small wood
I saw a squirrel gathering acorns in a **grove**.

harmlessly (härm′lĭs lē) adv. without danger
He fell from his sled and landed **harmlessly** in a snowbank.

hurl (hûrl) v. to throw; fling
He **hurled** his spear at the tiger and ran for safety.

invent (ĭn vĕnt′) v. to discover; create
Thomas Edison **invented** the telephone.

merrily (mĕr′ĭ lē) adv. gaily; in a jolly manner
The children played **merrily** with their new toys.

panic (păn′ĭk) n. sudden fright; overpowering terror
Panic spread through the crowd when the elephant escaped; the **panic** was more dangerous than the elephant.

personal (pûr′sən əl) adj. one's own
This is not a library book; it is my **personal** property.

proper (prŏp′ ər) adj. correct; respectable
He hoped he was wearing the **proper** clothes for the party.

stoke (stōk) v. to tend a stove or furnace
She **stoked** the wood-burning stove early every morning.

tame (tām) adj. unafraid; not timid
The chickadees in my yard are so **tame**, they feed from my hand.

terror (tĕr′ər) n. fright; intense fear
The hunter looked with **terror** at the crouching tiger.

unflattering (ŭn flăt′ər ĭng) adj. uncomplimentary
Although I knew I was a poor speller, it was **unflattering** to be chosen last for the spelling bee.

volcanic (vŏl kăn′ĭk) adj. fiery
The owner of the store had such a **volcanic** temper that everyone was afraid of him.

This is your space. You may:
   a. draw a picture about the poem
   b. write a story
   c. write a poem
   d. write a paragraph
Use at least three key words for b, c, or d.

Comprehension Check

Check the answer.

1. Wilbur resembled

_____ a. a dinosaur
_____ b. an erupting volcano
_____ c. an angry tiger

2. Little Bright Water was

_____ a. a little Indian boy
_____ b. a bubbling brook
_____ c. Chief Thundercloud's daughter

3. Wilbur stoked his stove with

_____ a. firewood
_____ b. red peppers
_____ c. chili peppers
_____ d. coal

Fill in the blanks in the paragraph with the following words:

children ran away from him   his head   orange and red smoke
corn   he looked so ferocious   his nostrils

Wilbur, the lovable dragon, was hurt because _____. They were
                                                             (4)

afraid of him because _____. _____ poured
                                 (5)   (6)

from _____. One day Little Bright Water came along, carrying _____
           (7)   (8)

to feed the birds. Frightened by Wilbur, she threw the corn at _____.
                                                                (9)

10. This poem is mainly about

_____ a. how children learned to trust a friendly dragon
_____ b. how popcorn was invented
_____ c. how to tame a dragon

Think about: If you had a pet dragon, what could he do to improve your life? Answer in verse, if
               you like.

_____

_____

_____

_____

The Emperor's Robe

To a famous old Emperor, long, long ago,
Came two wicked tailors who bowed very low.
"We've come," stated one with a smirk and a smile,
"To make you a robe of unusual style.
The cloth we shall use (oh, it passes belief!)
Is invisible, Sire, to a rogue or a thief!
Only the good and the just and the kind
Can see it, the cloth is so ultra-refined!"
Said the Emperor, being a bit of a dunce,
"Make it at once!"

Those tailors, the craftiest pair on the globe,
Then went through the motions of making the robe.
They measured and cut and they snipped and they stitched
While the Court and the Emperor watched them, bewitched.
Not one in the palace was honest enough
To say: "There's no robe! It's a hoax! It's a bluff!"
Instead, they exclaimed with exuberant praise:
"Never has robe so enchanted our gaze!"
The Emperor thought (and most puzzled was he)
"Everyone's able to see it but me!
I mustn't admit it because if I do,
It means I'm a rogue or I'd see the robe, too!
And so I must use my invalu'ble head,
And **pretend** that I see it!" Aloud, then, he said:
"The robe is distinguished! (Be careful! Don't tear it!)
And since it's a robe of exceptional merit,
I'll wear it!"

Well, wear it he did. Dressed in nothing, complete,
The Emperor happily strutted the street
While two little pages, important and vain,
Hoisted aloft his invisible train.
Everyone cheered him with fervor and joy
Except little Peter, the butcherman's boy,
Who, having no personal axes to grind,
Stated the truth with an innocent mind.
Cried Peter in wonder unblemished with guile:
"The Emperor's wearing a beautiful smile!
And," he went on in a tone clear and small,
"That's ALL!"

Key Words

admit (ăd mit') v. to confess; acknowledge
I **admitted** to Uncle Jim that I had not yet read the book he sent me.

aloft (ə lôft') adv. in or into a high place
Aloft was a flag bearing a skull and crossbones.

bewitch (bĭ wĭch') v. to fascinate; charm
Bewitched by Cinderella's beauty, the prince asked her to dance.

bluff (blŭf) n. a misleading act
His promise to pay the rent the next day was just a **bluff**.

crafty (krăf'tē) adj. shrewd; cunning
The **craftiest** little pig made his house of bricks.

dunce (dŭns) n. a stupid person
She felt like a **dunce** because she didn't understand the question.

enchant (ĕn chănt') v. to cast a spell over; delight
The little girl was **enchanted** with her new dollhouse.

exuberant (ĕg zoo'bər ənt) adj. effusively enthusiastic
Ned was **exuberant** when the coach told him he had finally made the team.

fervor (fûr'vər) n. intense emotion; ardor
When the juggler finished his act, the crowd applauded with **fervor**.

globe (glōb) n. the earth
The **globe** we call earth is one of billions of planets in the universe.

guile (gīl) n. artifice; craftiness
He trusted his business partner because of his honesty and lack of **guile**.

hoax (hōks) n. a practical joke or fraud
The police suspected the telephone call was a **hoax**.

hoist (hoist) v. to raise or lift
The pirates **hoisted** the treasure chest onto their ship.

invaluable (ĭn val′yoō ə bəl) adj. priceless
The owner of the ancient Egyptian vase said he wouldn't sell it—it was **invaluable**.

motion (mō′shən) n. a gesture or movement
Although the room looked empty, John noticed a **motion** behind the draperies.

page (pāj) n. a boy in attendance at court
The prince ordered his **page** to deliver the message immediately.

rogue (rōg) n. dishonest person; scoundrel
Rogues had broken into the house and stolen all the wedding presents.

smirk (smûrk) n. a simper; an affected smile
The teacher's pet **smirked** when he was chosen to lead the spelling bee.

strut (strŭt) v. to swagger; walk pompously
Leading the circus parade, the band **strutted** down Main Street.

unblemished (ŭn blĕm′ĭshd) adj. unimpaired; without a flaw
In the trunk I found an antique doll, its face **unblemished** by time.

Comprehension Check

Check the answer.

1. The tailors were

    ____a. honest laborers
    ____b. crafty thieves
    ____c. skilled garment makers
    ____d. friends of the emperor

2. The tailors promised to make

    ____a. a beautiful robe
    ____b. a fine 3-piece suit
    ____c. a royal toga

3. The emperor could best be described as

    ____a. very clever
    ____b. simple-minded
    ____c. tall and handsome

Fill in the blanks in the paragraph with the following words:

    thieves and rogues   pretend   admit   invisible

The cloth was _____ because it didn't exist. The people wouldn't _____
                    (4)   (5)
their inability to see the robe because that would mean they were_____.
                                                                           (6)
They decided to _____ they could see the robe.
                                      (7)

8. It is clear that

    ____a. the emperor was wearing his elegant new robe
    ____b. the emperor was marching along without any clothes on
    ____c. the emperor looked silly

9. Peter was the only one who

    ____a. made fun of the emperor
    ____b. truthfully said that the emperor was nude
    ____c. thought the emperor was splendidly dressed

10. This poem is mainly about

    ____a. how two tailors made an unusual robe
    ____b. how two rogues made fools of everyone except a truthful boy
    ____c. a robe that only good people could see

Think about: How would you punish the tailors?

See if you can solve the crossword puzzle below. If you get stuck (or need help) review the key words for "The Emperor's Robe."

Across

1. A misleading act
4. A kind of shirt
6. A long robe
7. To make yarn or thread
10. You're right, that's _____
11. "A poem as lovely as a _____"
12. "I think that I shall never _____"
13. Delighted
15. I _____ a bad dream
16. Slippery as an _____
17. To cut
18. The tailors wished they could _____ their hoax.

Down

1. Charmed
2. Given temporarily
3. To connect
4. _____ tell the truth
5. The Emperor wasn't even wearing a _____
6. It stuck like _____
8. To make believe
9. A wish for something that is lacking
12. Unhappy
14. The tailors weren't wearing one of these
16. The letter N

The Honest Man

Diogenes the Scholar, wagered once a silver dollar
He could find an honest man if he but tried!
With this in view he started. Optimistic and light-hearted,
He began to search the country far and wide.

In time his eyes grew bleary and his dusty feet grew weary.
Dishonest were the faces which he scanned.
There were thieves and rogues a-many, but of honest men, not any.
It wasn't quite as easy as he'd planned!

Yet with sturdy heart and sinew he determined to continue,
So for years and years he trudged from place to place.
"I'm sure," he often pondered as he traveled and he wandered,
"I'm sure I'll some day see an honest face!"

Arriving at a river which he waded with a shiver,
He quickly reached the pebbled farther brink.
Then, thirsty from his travel, he knelt upon the gravel—
But he didn't cup his hands and take a drink!

No! Prouder than a Major, he cried out, "I've won my wager!"
His relief was great, his satisfaction vast.
And with undisguised affection he stared down at his **reflection**!
"I've found," he cried, "an honest man at last!"

Key Words

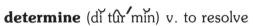

bleary (blîr′ē) adj. blurred; dimmed
Her eyes were **bleary** from studying so long for her Latin exam.

brink (brĭngk) n. the edge of land bordering on a body of water
When we came to the **brink** of the stream, we stopped to get a drink.

determine (dĭ tûr′mĭn) v. to resolve
She **determined** that she would join the space program as soon as she finished college.

optimistic (ŏp′tə mĭs tic) adj. expecting a favorable outcome
He was **optimistic** about his chances of getting a scholarship.

ponder (pŏn′dər) v. to consider carefully
The judge said he would need a few days to **ponder** his decision.

reflection (rĭ flĕk′shən) n. a mirrored image
Noticing his **reflection** in a store window, the man straightened his shoulders and pulled in his stomach.

rogue (rōg) n. a scoundrel or rascal
They had given their money to a **rogue** who promised to fix their roof, then left town.

scan (skăn) v. to examine or look closely
The prisoner **scanned** the courtroom, looking for members of his family.

scholar (skŏl′ər) n. a learned person
After the **scholar** graduated from college, she decided to go to England for further study.

Comprehension Check

Check the answer.

1. Diogenes was looking for

   ____a. a new restaurant
   ____b. silver dollars
   ____c. dishonest people
   ____d. an honest man
   ____e. fossils

2. Diogenes looked for an honest person

   ____a. in the closet
   ____b. at the bank
   ____c. everywhere he went
   ____d. in schools and universities

Fill in the blanks in the paragraph with the following words:

   thieves   an honest man   everywhere   reflection   a scholar

Diogenes was _____. He was looking for _____. He found
             (3)   (4)

many _____ but no honest man. He searched _____
         (5)   (6)

but was unsuccessful until he saw his _____.
                                          (7)

8. Diogenes could best be described as

   ____a. lazy
   ____b. silly
   ____c. dishonest
   ____d. determined

9. In this poem it is clear that

   ____a. there are not many honest people
   ____b. Diogenes liked to travel
   ____c. people see their reflections in rivers

10. This poem is mainly about

   ____a. a man's travels
   ____b. a man's search for an honest person
   ____c. a man's search for silver

Think about: How many honest people do you know? How can you tell they are honest?

The Magical Hat

Patrick was hunting, one Halloween day,
Through a trunkful of treasures long hidden away.
When much to the pleasure and profit of Pat,
He came on a wonderful magical hat.

Well, quite as if this were his usual habit,
He put in his hand, and he drew out a rabbit.
Pleased, but not thrilled into shivers and chills,
Pat muttered: "That trick is as old as the hills!"
Then thoughtfully scratching his little red head,
"I think I will pull out some **people**!" he said.
And he did! From that hat so imposing and tall,
He pulled out a lady in bonnet and shawl.
A dignified man and a spinster came next,
And one or two more whose expressions were vexed.
"I," said the lady, "was having a nap!"
"And I," said a man, "was at dinner, young chap!"
"I," sniffed the spinster, "was feeding my cats!"
"We **hate**," they all cried, "to be pulled out of hats!"
With this, looking ever so grumpy and glum,
They jumped in the hat out of which they had come,
And—pfffftt!—they all vanished! "Now, that," approved Patrick,
"Is what I would call a remarkable hat trick!"

Key Words

approve (ə prōōv´) v. to have a favorable opinion of
She was glad her parents **approved** of the young man she wanted to marry.

bonnet (bŏn´ĭt) n. a hat tied on with ribbons under the chin
The father helped his little girl put on her coat and **bonnet**.

chap (chăp) n. a man or boy; a fellow
A **chap** sitting behind me at the baseball game asked me if I had a match.

dignified (dĭg nə fīd´) adj. stately; having dignity
The school was run by a **dignified** white-haired woman who always wore black.

expression (ĕk sprĕsh´ən) n. a look that conveys a special feeling
Although my father didn't scold me, I could tell by his **expression** that he was disappointed in me.

glum (glŭm) adj. gloomy; cheerless
I knew my father would be **glum** when he saw my report card.

grumpy (grŭm´pē) adj. fretful; irritable
Dad looked so **grumpy** when he came home from work, I decided to show him my marks some other time.

imposing (ĭm pō´zĭng) adj. impressive; awesome
A tall, **imposing** man opened the door of the mansion and asked me whom I wanted to see.

mutter (mŭt′ər) v. to utter in low, indistinct tones; grumble
"Now where did I put my glasses?" Grandmother **muttered**.

pffftt (pffftt) interj. an explosive interjection used when something suddenly disappears
One minute there was a bird sitting on the magician's hand, the next minute—**pffftt**!—it was gone.

profit (prŏf′ĭt) n. a gain; a benefit
Richard found his experience as a camp counselor a **profit** when he had children of his own.

remarkable (rĭ mär′kə bəl) adj. extraordinary; uncommon
It was **remarkable** that the girl could ski so well with only one leg.

shawl (shôl) n. a loose covering for the neck and shoulders
The old woman's **shawl** didn't look warm enough for such a cold day.

sniff (snĭf) v. to inhale a short, audible breath through the nose, expressing contempt or doubt
The spoiled princess **sniffed** at her presents and said what she really wanted was a unicorn.

spinster (spĭn′stər) n. an unmarried woman
Although Emily had had many chances to marry, she chose to remain a **spinster**.

vanish (văn′ĭsh) v. to disappear quickly
When she turned to thank the man who had saved her daughter from drowning, he had **vanished**.

vexed (vĕkst) adj. annoyed; irritated
Mother was **vexed** with me because I hadn't told her I would be late for dinner.

Comprehension Check

Check four (½ point each).

1-2. Patrick was able to pull out of his hat

_____ a. a bathtub   _____ e. a little boy
_____ b. a spinster   _____ f. a dignified man
_____ c. a parrot   _____ g. a lady
_____ d. a rabbit   _____ h. three yellow scarves

Check the answer.

3. Why was the spinster unhappy to be pulled out of the hat?

_____ a. She didn't look well in hats.
_____ b. She was feeding her cats at the time.
_____ c. She had just gone to bed.

4. Why was the man vexed with Patrick?

_____ a. He was taking a bath.
_____ b. He was cooking dinner.
_____ c. He was eating his dinner.

Fill in the blanks in the paragraph with the following words:

a magical hat   a rabbit   people   Halloween

Patrick was looking for treasures on _____. He found _____.
(5)   (6)
Patrick's old trick was to pull out _____. Patrick's wonderful new trick was to pull
(7)
out _____.
(8)

Check the answer.

9. How did the people leave Patrick?

_____ a. They took a plane.
_____ b. They got on a bus.
_____ c. They jumped back in the hat.
_____ d. They went out the back door.

10. This poem is mainly about

_____ a. Patrick and his friends
_____ b. how magicians perform tricks
_____ c. a magical hat on Halloween
_____ d. a spinster, a lady, and a man

Think about: If you were a magician, what tricks would you perform? Answer in verse, if you like.

Meranda

Long ago, and far below the sea's gigantic gale,
Meranda lived—a mermaid with a most becoming tail.
Her face was sweet and merry, and her voice, enchanting, very,
As it mingled, light and airy, with the ocean's somber scale.

King Neptune heard and was so stirred, he called his wizards three.
"I want to keep Meranda's song! It must not die!" said he.
"Come, wizard and magician! Show your skill and your ambition,
And grant the wish I'm wishin'! Catch this lovely song for me!"

The wisest of the wizards did not have to ponder long.
Said he with verve, "A shell will serve to hold Meranda's song!"
His brothers cried, "Be quiet! You're a fool! You can't deny it!"
But the king replied, "Let's **try** it! This will prove him right or wrong!"

Meranda, then, began again her captivating art.
She held a shell and sang to it while Neptune stood apart.
She charmed the king completely with the tune she trilled so sweetly—
And the shell retained it neatly in its iridescent heart.

Go find a shell and listen well and tell me what you hear.
Though wave and wind have dimmed and thinned that singing, once so clear,
Through walls of pink and yellow you will hear the ocean's cello . . .
And a murmur, soft and mellow, will whisper in your ear.

Key Words

ambition (ăm bĭsh′ən) n. zeal
Hard work and **ambition** helped her to get through medical school.

becoming (bē kŭm′ĭng) adj. pleasing; good-looking
She was wearing a **becoming** dress with a matching jacket.

captivating (kăp′tĭ vā′tĭng) adj. fascinating
My new friend was a **captivating** girl with a twinkle in her eye and a warm personality.

cello (chĕl′ō) n. a musical instrument
The musician's **cello** looked like a large violin.

charm (chärm) v. to please; delight
The little boy's honesty **charmed** the old lady; he said he hadn't meant to run through her flower garden.

completely (kəm plēt′lē) adv. entirely; totally
After the relay race, she was **completely** exhausted.

deny (dĭ nī′) v. to disclaim; declare untrue
Did they **deny** they had broken the window with their baseball?

dim (dĭm) v. to become fainter
At curtain time the lights were **dimmed**; the play was about to begin.

enchanting (ĕn chănt′ĭng) adj. charming; fascinating
We took many pictures of the **enchanting** Japanese gardens we saw during our trip.

gigantic (jī găn′tĭk) adj. huge
His mother had made a **gigantic** birthday cake.

iridescent (ĭ′ rĭ dĕs′ ənt) adj. pearly; rainbow-like
Her opal ring had an **iridescent** shine.

mellow (mĕl′ō) adj. tender; sweet
His guitar provided a **mellow** background for her folk song.

mingle (mĭng′gəl) v. to mix; blend
Children **mingled** with grown-ups at the science museum.

murmur (mûr′mər) n. a soft sound
She was awakened by the **murmur** of voices outside her room.

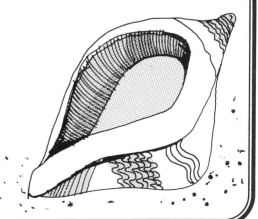

ponder (pŏn′dər) v. to think over; consider
The President said he would **ponder** the problem over the weekend.

retain (rē tān′) v. to keep
She **retained** her interest in dinosaurs and read every book she could find on the subject.

serve (sûrv) v. to be useful
A pillowcase will **serve** as a laundry bag.

skill (skĭl) n. ability
It took a lot of **skill** to make the model airplane.

somber (sŏm′bər) adj. solemn; grave
The father said in a **somber** voice that he had lost his job.

stir (stûr) v. to impress; affect
The audience at Symphony Hall was **stirred** by the young violinist.

trill (trĭl) v. to warble
A song sparrow **trilled** sweetly in the garden outside my window.

verve (vûrv) n. enthusiasm
The crowd cheered with **verve** when the home team finally won the basketball game.

This is your space. You may:
    a. draw a picture about the poem
    b. write a story
    c. write a poem
    d. write a paragraph
Use at least three key words for b, c, or d.

Comprehension Check

Check the answer.

1. King Neptune asked his wizards
   - _____ a. to go golfing
   - _____ b. how to save Meranda's song
   - _____ c. to do tricks

2. Meranda saved her song by
   - _____ a. taping it on her recorder
   - _____ b. singing it into a shell
   - _____ c. writing it in the sand

Fill in the blanks in the paragraph with the following words:

> charmed enchanting shell sang song tune

Meranda's voice was _____. King Neptune wanted to catch Meranda's
(3)

_____. Meranda held a shell and _____ into it. The king was
(4)   (5)

_____ by the _____ she trilled.
(6)   (7)

9. If you find a shell and listen well, you will hear
   - _____ a. "The Star-Spangled Banner"
   - _____ b. a whistling sound
   - _____ c. a murmuring whisper

10. This poem is mainly about
    - _____ a. a contest between a wizard and a magician
    - _____ b. how the mermaid got her tail
    - _____ c. how King Neptune kept Meranda's song

Think about: Do you think the story of this poem really happened? Why or why not?

_____

_____

_____

_____

_____

_____

The Mouse and the Weasel

Murphy, my dear, was a bright little mouse
Who chanced to be born in an Irishman's house
Which furnished him food to his merry content,
(Without his host's knowledge, much less his consent!)
So Murphy was happy until, came the day
When his host packed his trunk and went riding away.
"Faith and Begorry!" our Murphy said he,
"He didn't make any provisions for **me**!
Bejabbers, how selfish some people can be!"
(Having lived all his life in an Irishman's house,
He squeaked with an accent, did Murphy, the mouse.)

In a week he was thin, and so, feeling glum,
He scampered outdoors in search of a crumb.
His little tail twitched, and his little nose tweaked.
"Here's a bin with some corn at the bottom!" he squeaked.
"And faith, here's a hole at the base of the bin
Which is just the right size for a mouse to get in, **if he's thin**!"

Once in the barrel, he ate and he ate!
Yes, he ate with such greed that he **doubled his weight**!
Having gobbled his fill, he then found to his fright
That **he couldn't get out**! The hole was too tight!

He was stuck, (being now very much on the stout side)
With his tail on the inside, his head on the outside!
A weasel came by, and he stopped for a stare.
"Well, well!" he remarked with a critical air.
"Your hunger let greediness open the throttle,
So now you are stuck like a cork in a bottle!
If you want to get out by the hole you got in,
You must starve till again you're as thin as a pin!"
"I know it," said Murphy. "I do, sir, indeed!
I've learned **moderation is wiser than greed**!"

With this pleasing moral we finish our story . . .
Faith and bejabbers, be gum and begorry!

43

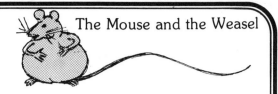

Key Words

accent (ăk′sĕnt) n. speech pattern or pronunciation
I could tell by the man's **accent** that he was an Englishman.

bin (bĭn) n. a box or storage place
By the end of the winter, their coal **bin** was almost empty.

chance (chăns) v. to happen or occur by chance
It **chanced** that he was going to the same summer camp I was.

consent (kən sĕnt′) n. agreement; approval
"You shouldn't have borrowed my camera without my **consent**," I said to my brother.

content (kən tĕnt′) adj. satisfied; not wanting anything else
On a rainy summer day, she was **content** to read or work on her stamp collection.

critical (krĭt′ĭ kəl) adj. judicial; judgmental
Giving herself a **critical** look in the mirror, she saw that her skirt was too long.

double (dŭb′əl) v. to make twice as great
In less than a year she had **doubled** the earnings from her paper route.

furnish (fûr′nĭsh) v. to provide; supply
If you will **furnish** the sandwiches, I'll bring cookies and lemonade.

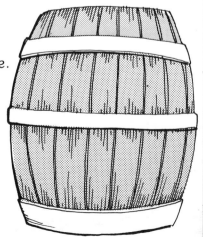

glum (glŭm) adj. gloomy; morose
The students looked **glum** when they saw their Latin assignment.

gobble (gŏb′əl) v. to eat hastily; gulp
The man **gobbled** his meal as if he were starving.

greediness (grēd′ĕ nĕs) n. an unreasonable desire for food; gluttony
Because of the man's **greediness**, there was barely enough food left for his family.

host (hōst) n. a person who has guests
Our **host** greeted us at the door of his new house.

merry (mĕr′ē) adj. full of cheerfulness; laughingly gay
With a **merry** twinkle in her eye, my mother said she had a surprise for me.

moderation (mŏd ə rā′shən) n. restraint; avoidance of extremes
A driver who uses **moderation** goes neither too fast nor too slow.

moral (mŏr′əl) n. the practical lesson in a story or experience
The **moral** of the story was that people in glass houses shouldn't throw stones.

remark (rĭ märk′) v. to say; comment
Someone **remarked** that Monday was a holiday.

scamper (skăm′pər) v. to run quickly
As soon as the cat saw the dog, it **scampered** up a tree.

search (sûrch) n. a careful investigation
The **search** ended happily when the missing boys were found asleep in a cave.

stare (stâr) n. an intent gaze, with the eyes wide open
My mother just stood there with a **stare** when she saw the mess.

stout (stout) adj. fat; overweight
Her uncle was so **stout**, he had trouble tying his shoelaces.

throttle (thrŏt´l) n. a valve that regulates the flow of fuel
"Hurry! Step on the **throttle**!" the woman cried to the cab driver. "My plane leaves in 20 minutes!"

tweak (twēk) v. to twist; twitch
The horse's ears **tweaked** as he patiently waited for his dinner pail.

twitch (twĭch) v. a quick jerky movement of the body
If your eyelids **twitch** when you're asleep, you are having a dream.

Pretend you have a pet mouse and in this box write a letter to a friend. Use at least three key words.

Comprehension Check

Check the answer.

1. Murphy's problem took place

   ____a. in a barrel
   ____b. in America
   ____c. in a cellar
   ____d. in a mouse house

2. The weasel's plan was to

   ____a. cut a hole in the barrel
   ____b. put Murphy on a diet
   ____c. roll the barrel downhill until it broke
   ____d. gnaw on the hole until it was bigger

Fill in the blanks in the paragraph with the following words:

   host   meals   barrel   corn

Murphy ate his _____ at an Irishman's house. Unfortunately, Murphy's _____
(3)   (4)

moved away. Murphy was starving until he found food in a _____. He
(5)

couldn't get out because he ate too much _____.
(6)

7-8. Check the two statements that are **not** true.

   ____a. Murphy loved to eat.
   ____b. Murphy was always dieting.
   ____c. Murphy lived in an Irishman's house.
   ____d. The weasel and Murphy lived together.

9. The lesson that Murphy learned was:

   ____a. Overeating causes stomachaches.
   ____b. Be careful whom you trust.
   ____c. Don't play in barrels.
   ____d. Eat only what you need.

10. This story is mainly about

   ____a. Mickey and Minnie Mouse
   ____b. Irish people
   ____c. the importance of using moderation
   ____d. staying out of tight spots

Think about the saying, "Look before you leap." It means _____

_____.

Essay on Mules

There once was a crotchety little gray mule
Which, weary of hauling his load,
Stopped short in a shadow invitingly cool,
And sat down by the side of the road.
His owner commanded the creature to rise.
He prodded, he pushed, and he cussed;
But the little mule, lazily blinking his eyes,
Just sat on his tail in the dust.
A passerby said as he paused in the street,
"How small is the power of force!
Permit me, my friend! I can bring to his feet
That stubborn excuse for a horse!"
Did he beat the poor beast? No, indeed he did not!
He showed him a carrot or two,
And this caused the mule to get up on the spot,
As his owner had wanted him to.
Now, **people** are mulish—and so, if you're wise,
You'll learn as you travel the years,
That to badger or bluster (or even advise)
Causes humans to lay back their ears.
Make tactful persuasion your every-day rule.
Suggest, if you must. Don't **command**.
Then you'll find that the crankiest two-legged mule
Will shortly eat out of your hand!

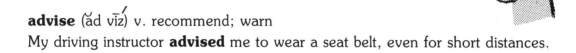

Key Words

advise (ăd vīz′) v. recommend; warn
My driving instructor **advised** me to wear a seat belt, even for short distances.

badger (băj′ər) v. pester; nag
"Stop **badgering** me, children!" the mother said, losing her patience.

bluster (blŭs′tər) v. to talk with noisy violence; bully
The wolf tried to **bluster** his way into the little pig's house.

command (kə mănd′) v. to order
The general **commanded** his troops to cease firing until further orders.

cranky (krăngk′ē) adj. irritable; ill-natured
Uncle Henry was **cranky** every morning until he had his coffee.

crotchety (krŏch′ĭ tē) adj. grouchy
Granddad was feeling **crotchety** because he couldn't find his glasses.

cuss (kŭs) v. to swear
My father **cussed** when he got a flat tire on the way to the beach.

excuse (ĭk skyōōs′) n. poor substitute
Does that yapping **excuse** for a watchdog belong to your family?

force (fôrs) n. physical coercion
The police had to use **force** to break up the fight at the ball game.

invitingly (ĭn vī′tĭng lē) adv. attractively; alluringly
The sandwiches and cold lemonade looked **invitingly** refreshing after our long tennis match.

mulish (myōō′lĭsh) adj. obstinate; stubborn
My **mulish** brother said he wouldn't come with us to Grandmother's unless he could bring his pet snake.

pause (pôz) v. to stop briefly
I **paused** when I came to the fork in the road.

passerby (păs′ər bī′) n. a person passing by
A **passerby** noticed the house was on fire and called the fire department.

permit (pûr mĭt′) v. to allow
"Would you **permit** me to help you across the street?" the young girl said to the blind woman.

persuasion (pər swā′zhən) n. reasoning; inducement
Due to my **persuasion**, my friend changed her mind and signed up for the swimming team.

power (pou′ər) n. strength
The giant had the **power** of ten men.

prod (prŏd) v. to poke; jab
I **prodded** him with my elbow to get his attention.

stubborn (stŭb′ ərn) adj. obstinate
The **stubborn** man insisted he was all right, even though he had a deep cut in his forehead.

suggest (sə jĕst′) v. to offer for consideration or action
It was a lovely day. Dad **suggested** that we pack a lunch and go for a hike.

tactful (tăkt′fəl) adj. considerate; sensitive
When I spilled the gravy, my **tactful** aunt said the tablecloth was washable.

weary (wẽr′ ē) adj. tired
We were weary after our long hike through the woods.

This is your space. Do your own thing, using at least three key words.

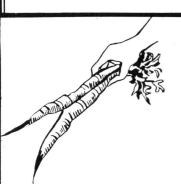

Comprehension Check

Check the answer.

1. The owner wanted the mule to

    ____a. eat carrots
    ____b. get up and get going
    ____c. be friendly to passersby
    ____d. give him a ride

2. The passerby's plan succeeded because

    ____a. he knew how to talk to animals
    ____b. whipping accomplishes more than pushing
    ____c. the mule responded to the reward

Check the statement that is **not** true.

3. ____a. Mules are usually stubborn.
    ____b. People don't like to be told what to do.
    ____c. Tactful persuasion is a good way to get cooperation.
    ____d. Animals and people eat carrots to improve their minds and bodies.

Fill in the blanks in the paragraph with the following words:

      stubborn   sat down   prodded and pushed   motivated

The little mule _____ and wouldn't move. His owner _____,
                   (4)   (5)
but the little mule was _____. People can be _____ by rewards.
                          (6)   (7)

Check two.

8-9. A reward system
    ____a. works all the time
    ____b. is a good method for getting cooperation
    ____c. works only with adults
    ____d. solves all your problems
    ____e. works only with children
    ____f. works some of the time
    ____g. works only with animals

10. This story is mainly about

    ____a. why people and mules like carrots
    ____b. how best to treat other people
    ____c. how to get a·mule to move

Think about: Tell how you could get your sister or brother to do your chores for a week.

The Oyster

Beneath the sea so wild and rude,
A melancholy oyster
Once dwelt in lonely solitude
Inside his clammy cloister.

He didn't own a single "fin!"
Poor fish! With sad emotion
He envied all his scornful kin
That swam the stormy ocean.

The oyster knew he was despised
By all of his relations.
He was, you might say, "oystracized"
By upper-crust crustaceans!

And then it happened, one fine day,
A gritty granule nicked him.
It hurt him more than words can say—
O, how it plagued its victim!

Unable to dislodge the grain,
He left it where he found it,
But goaded by his grievous pain,
He built a **pearl** around it!

Now he was rich! The tidings flew,
And soon his rank was stellar.
All fin-land knew (and envied, too)
This little Rocky-feller.

So, reader, don't give up and quit
When life seems sad and shoddy.
Remember this: A little **grit**
Is good for everybody!

Key Words

befall (bǐ fôl´) v. to happen
It **befell** that there was a blizzard that night, so the town meeting was held a week later.

clammy (klăm´ē) adj. cold and damp
His wet boots felt **clammy** when he put them on again.

cloister (kloi´stər) n. a quiet, secluded place
The boy had built a hut in the woods; it was his private **cloister** where he could read and dream.

crustacean (krŭ stā´shən) n. sea animal with a hard shell
Lobsters and other **crustaceans** were caught in traps set by the fishermen.

dislodge (dǐs lŏj´) v. to force out; remove
His mother used a needle to **dislodge** the splinter in his finger.

dwell (dwĕl) v. to live or reside
The wizard **dwelt** in the land of Oz.

emotion (ǐ mō´shən) n. a strong or agitated feeling
When he heard that his family had not been hurt in the earthquake, an **emotion** of great relief swept over him.

envy (ĕn´vē) v. to feel discontented at the good fortune of another
John couldn't help **envying** his best friend, who had been invited to go surfing in California.

fin (fǐn) n. Slang. a five-dollar bill
Back in the 1930's a man was lucky to get a **fin** for a day's work.

goad (gōd) v. urge, prod
Goaded by his pals, the boy had climbed to the top of the tower.

granule (grăn′yo͞ol) n. a small particle
The mother swept up the spilled **granules** of cornmeal.

grievous (grē′vəs) adj. severe; serious
It is a **grievous** mistake to leave a pet in a hot car with the windows rolled up.

grit (grĭt) n. unyielding determination; pluck
She had too much **grit** to let the accident ruin her life; someday she knew she would teach from a wheelchair.

gritty (grĭt′ē) adj. sandy
The spinach was **gritty** because it hadn't been thoroughly washed.

kin (kĭn) n. one's relatives
All his **kin** met once a year for a picnic on the Fourth of July.

melancholy (mĕl′ən kŏl′ē) adj. sad; mournful
The young man was feeling **melancholy** because his dog had died.

nick (nĭk) v. to cut into
My father **nicked** his chin while he was shaving.

ostracize (ŏs′trə sīz) v. to exclude, by general consent, from society
When it was learned that the boy had won by cheating, he was **ostracized** by his friends.

57

plague (plāg) v. to trouble; torment
The poison ivy sores **plagued** him for two weeks.

rank (răngk) n. relative position or standing
Her **rank** was third in the state's tennis competition.

relation (rĭ lā′shən) n. relative
She hoped some day to visit her **relations** in France.

Rockefeller, John D. 1839-1937. Wealthy American industrialist and philanthropist
Tom used to dream about what he would do with his money if he were as rich as **Rockefeller**.

scornful (skôrn′fəl) adj. contemptuous; disdainful
"Do you call that minnow a fish?" his big brother asked in a **scornful** tone.

shoddy (shŏd′ē) adj. inferior
Because of **shoddy** workmanship, the bridge had collapsed.

solitude (sŏl′ĭ tōōd) n. the state of being alone; seclusion
In the **solitude** of her bedroom, she wrote in her diary every night.

upper crust (ŭp′ər krust) n. the highest social class
Only members of the **upper crust** could hope to attend the royal ball.

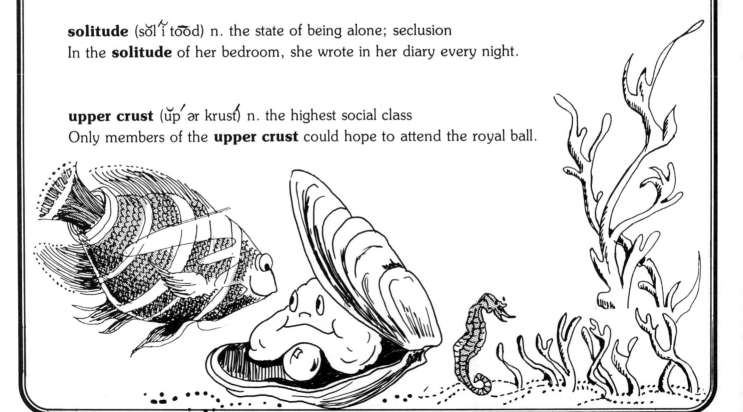

Comprehension Check

1-3. A pun is the humorous use of words that sound alike but have different meanings. Which of the words below are puns?

Check three.

    ____a. oystracized
    ____b. gritty granule
    ____c. Rocky-feller
    ____d. clammy cloister
    ____e. fin-land
    ____f. grievous pain

Check the answer.

4. The oyster was sad because

    ____a. he didn't have any money in his bank account
    ____b. he was despised by all his relatives
    ____c. his family had all been made into Oysters Rockefeller

5. What did the oyster do about the grit?

    ____a. He made some for breakfast.
    ____b. He endured it.
    ____c. He built a pearl around it.
    ____d. He took a shower.

Fill in the blanks in the paragraph with the following words:

        uncomfortable   grievous   scornful   melancholy

The _____ oyster lived beneath the sea. He became _____ when
          (6)   (7)
a grain of sand lodged in his shell. Because of his _____ pain, he built a pearl
                                                          (8)
around it. The other crustaceans were no longer _____.
                                                          (9)

10. This poem is mainly about

    ____a. how an oyster was ostracized by his relatives
    ____b. how precious pearls are made from a piece of grit inside an oyster
    ____c. an unhappy oyster

Think about: Make up a pun about a very cold baby dog, using the word *Popsicle*. Make up a pun about a canary, using the word *cheap*.

Peter the Puppet

Peter was a puppet. When you pulled the proper string,
He'd leap and prance or jog or dance or do the Highland fling,
Or turn a lively somersault, or tap a nimble shoe;
In fact there wasn't anything that Peter couldn't do!

Now, Melinda, who received the little puppet as a gift,
Was in a mood extremely rude. She looked at him and sniffed.
Then pulling **all** his strings **at once** (this wasn't kind a bit!),
She so upset the precious pet, he had a puppet fit!

Putting on an act that almost tore him limb from limb,
The puppet danced and tumbled with excruciating vim!
He jigged a jig that loosed his wig! He danced a lovely waltz,
And finished with a somersault to end all somersaults!

His dance was done, his jig was up, his Highland fling was flung!
Poor Peter lay upon the floor—and oh, he felt unstrung!
Melinda was remorseful, and her pretty eyes grew wet
As Peter sprawled, forlorn and bald, his strings a tangled net.

Melinda had him mended (he was not completely wrecked!),
And after that, she treated him with kindness and respect.
For puppets are like **people**. Both will "dance" for you, in fact,
If only you'll observe the rule of gentleness and tact.

Key Words

excruciating (ĕk skroō'shē āt'ĭng) adj. intensely painful; tormenting
She asked her children to play quietly because she had an **excruciating** headache.

extremely (ĕk strēm'lē) adv. in the highest degree; very greatly
When my mother got home, she was **extremely** pleased to find the house neat and the table set.

fit (fĭt) n. a sudden attack; a convulsion
She nearly had a **fit** when she learned her best friend was moving to another state.

forlorn (fôr lôrn') adj. wretched; pitiful
The policeman asked the **forlorn** little girl if she was lost.

Highland fling (hī'land flĭng) n. a Scottish folk dance
Our cousin from Scotland offered to teach us the **Highland fling**.

jig (jĭg) v. to bob up and down jerkily; dance a jig
When my baby brother heard the lively tune, he began to **jig** in his playpen.

limb (lĭm) n. an arm or leg
He could hardly feel his **limbs**, they were so numb after his swim in the icy lake.

lively (līv'lē) adj. full of life; animated
The **lively** kitten was batting a ball of yarn around the room.

mood (moōd) n. a temporary state of mind or feeling
My **mood** changed from happy to sad when I heard of my grandfather's illness.

nimble (nĭm′bəl) adj. quick and agile; deft
A family of monkeys was swinging **nimbly** through the trees in the jungle.

prance (prăns) v. to move in a lively manner; strut
The kitten **pranced** around the room, chasing the bouncing ball.

precious (prĕsh′əs) adj. cherished; beloved
His most **precious** possession was his collection of fossils.

proper (prŏp′ər) adj. appropriate; suitable
When Mother lit the candles on the cake, I knew this was the **proper** moment to make a wish.

receive (rĭ sēv′) v. to acquire or get something
Of all the presents the child **received**, she liked the rocking horse best.

remorseful (rĭ môrs′fəl) adj. regretful for past misdeeds
Tommy was **remorseful** when he realized he had hurt his brother's feelings.

respect (rĭ spĕkt′) n. a feeling of esteem; deferential regard
Because of his **respect** for his grandfather, Fred often went to him for advice.

sniff (snĭf) v. to inhale a short audible breath; show contempt
When Susan tried to make up with her friend, the girl just **sniffed** and walked away.

sprawl (sprôl) v. to sit or lie with the body spread out awkwardly
The little boy was **sprawled** on the floor, playing with his toy trains.

tact (tăkt) n. the ability to say or do the kind thing; diplomacy
Noticing that Tom's eyes were red, the teacher had the **tact** not to ask him why he was late.

unstrung (ŭn'strŭng) adj. having strings loosened; unnerved; upset
After spending the day taking care of my neighbor's twins, I felt **unstrung**.

upset (ŭp sĕt) v. to distress; disturb
It **upset** me when I didn't find my diary in its usual place.

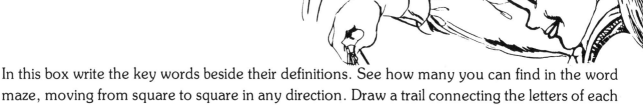

In this box write the key words beside their definitions. See how many you can find in the word maze, moving from square to square in any direction. Draw a trail connecting the letters of each word.

```
L  P  R  T  C  P
I  V  A  A  T  R
E  N  C  E  O  P
L  Y  L  L  R  E
E  U  O  I  M  B
F  S  R  M  E  R
```

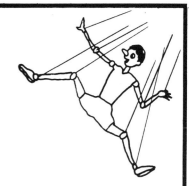

Definitions	Key Words
1. an arm or leg	_____
2. full of life	_____
3. to move in a lively manner	_____
4. suitable	_____
5. regretful	_____
6. diplomacy	_____

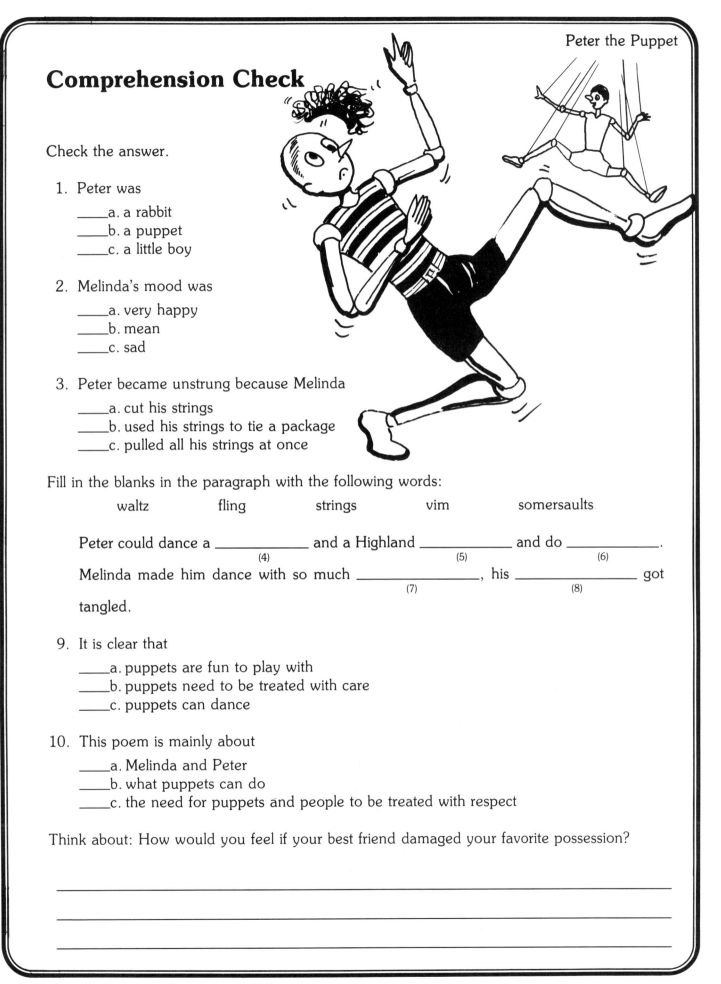

Comprehension Check

Peter the Puppet

Check the answer.

1. Peter was

   ____a. a rabbit
   ____b. a puppet
   ____c. a little boy

2. Melinda's mood was

   ____a. very happy
   ____b. mean
   ____c. sad

3. Peter became unstrung because Melinda

   ____a. cut his strings
   ____b. used his strings to tie a package
   ____c. pulled all his strings at once

Fill in the blanks in the paragraph with the following words:

waltz   fling   strings   vim   somersaults

Peter could dance a _____ and a Highland _____ and do _____.
              (4)   (5)   (6)
Melinda made him dance with so much _____, his _____ got
                                     (7)   (8)
tangled.

9. It is clear that

   ____a. puppets are fun to play with
   ____b. puppets need to be treated with care
   ____c. puppets can dance

10. This poem is mainly about

   ____a. Melinda and Peter
   ____b. what puppets can do
   ____c. the need for puppets and people to be treated with respect

Think about: How would you feel if your best friend damaged your favorite possession?

_____

_____

_____

The Pied Piper of Hamelin

There once was a village much troubled with rats.
They frightened the children and fought with the cats.
They ate all in sight, did these rats of renown . . .
Then at last a young piper came strolling to town.
Said he to the townfolk: "These rodents are bold,
But I'll rid you of them for a bagful of gold!"
"Very good!" Mayor Thomas replied from his lawn,
"I'll pay you the gold when the last rat is gone!"

The piper, well pleased with the bargain he'd made,
Lifted his flute and he played and he played.
Bewitched by his piping so merry and weird,
From cellar and attic the big rats appeared.
They leaped out of corners and crannies and rocks,
They sprang out of cupboards and climbed out of crocks.
Gray ones and black ones, fat ones and lean,
They followed him off and were never more seen.
But when he returned and demanded his pay,
Mayor Thomas spoke rudely: "Be off! Go away!"

At midnight the piper came back to the street,
Playing a tune unbelievably sweet.
Small sleepy children and tottering tots
Hearing his melody, crept from their cots!

They stole from their homes, this pajama'd parade,
And followed the piper away as he played.

Next morning, "Alas!" cried the mothers to Thomas,
"Would you had paid him, and honored your promise!"
Meanwhile, the children trudged on, half asleep;
So weary were they, some were starting to weep.
By the time that the piper had reached his home-cave,
The tots were so fretful, they couldn't behave.
They quarreled and wrangled and hollered and ki-yied
Until the poor piper was less **pied** than pie-eyed.
Indeed, the poor fellow who'd lived all alone,
Now found that his time was no longer his own.
The children, poor dears, gave him no time for practice,
And this being so, he grew prickly as cactus.
Busy all day was the once-merry piper,
Washing a face, or changing a di'per!
Cooking their meals, and consoling their wails,
He now had no leisure for playing his scales.
"They all need their mothers!" he muttered. "Alack!
For my sake and theirs, I must hurry them back!"
So homeward to Hamelin he led them, one day—
And the town was so thankful, they doubled his pay!

Key Words

The Pied Piper of Hamelin

alack (ə lăḱ) interj.
alas (ə lăś) interj. exclamations of regret or sorrow
"**Alas** and **alack**!" cried the witch. "I've lost my magic shoes!"

bewitch (bĭ wĭch́) v. to place under one's spell by magic; cast a spell over
After Sleeping Bearuty was **bewitched**, she awoke when the prince kissed her.

cactus (kăḱ təs) n. a plant with prickly stems
My aunt told me not to touch her Christmas **cactus**—I might prick my finger.

console (kən sōĺ) v. to comfort
When Tommy cut his knee, his mother **consoled** him by buying him an ice-cream cone.

cranny (krăń ē) n. a small opening in a wall or rock; crevice
The man hid the gold in a **cranny** near the bottom of a stone wall.

crock (krŏk) n. an earthenware vessel or pot
The farmer's wife kept cornmeal in a **crock** in the cupboard.

fretful (frĕt́ fəl) adj. peevish; plaintive
After taking care of two **fretful** children all day, the baby sitter was worn out.

honor (ŏń ər) v. to pay when due; respect
He always **honored** his debts by paying them promptly.

ki-yi (kī́ yī́) v. Slang. to yelp shrilly
When the cat scratched the dog's nose, he howled and **ki-yied** as he ran back to his yard.

leisure (lḗ zhər) n. spare time; freedom from responsibility
The mother of the triplets seldom had the **leisure** to read a book or write a poem.

Pied Piper (pīd′pī′pər) German Legend. A piper who rid the town of rats by piping. When refused payment, he led away the children of the town.
Before the children went to bed, their father read them the story of the **Pied Piper**.

pie-eyed (pī′īd′) adj. Slang. cockeyed drunk
The wife complained that her husband had gotten **pie-eyed** at the party.

piper (pī′pər) n. one who plays a pipe consisting of a tube
In "Peter and the Wolf," the **piper** imitates the sound of a bird.

renown (rĭ noun′) n. fame; celebrity
When the boys found the buried treasure, they became **renowned** throughout the village.

scale (skāl) n. an ascending or descending series of tones
Every day after school, she practiced her **scales** on the piano.

steal (stēl) v. to move stealthily or unobtrusively
Early Christmas morning the children **stole** from their beds and peeked at the presents under the tree.

stroll (strōl) v. to walk at a leisurely pace
As we **strolled** through town, we stopped now and then to talk to our friends.

trudge (trŭj) v. to plod; walk laboriously
The little boy **trudged** upstairs, dragging his teddy bear behind him.

wail (wāl) v. to cry out plaintively
The child **wailed** when his balloon slipped out of his hand.

would (wŏŏd) past participle of verb *will*. expression of desire or wish; if only
"**Would** I were young again!" my grandfather says when he sees a pretty girl.

Comprehension Check

Check the answer.

1. The village of Hamelin had trouble with

   ____a. wildcats
   ____b. rats
   ____c. undisciplined children

2. The townsfolk solved the problem by

   ____a. hiring the Pied Piper as a baby-sitter
   ____b. hiring a lion tamer
   ____c. hiring the Pied Piper to bewitch the rats

3. The mayor paid the Pied Piper

   ____a. with gold
   ____b. with a certified check
   ____c. nothing

Fill in the blanks in the paragraph with the following words:

      merry   sleepy   unbelievably sweet   fretful   thankful

The _____ children heard the piper's _____ melody and followed
(4)   (5)

him. The tots were so _____ that the piper was no longer _____,
(6)   (7)

The town was _____ when the piper led the children home again.
(8)

9. The lesson the mayor learned was that

   ____a. debts should be honored
   ____b. pipers are good baby-sitters
   ____c. pipers can't be trusted

10. This poem is mainly about

   ____a. a dishonest mayor
   ____b. how to get rid of rats
   ____c. a piper who bewitched the children of Hamelin
   ____d. runaway children

Think about: Would you ever leave school with a stranger?

70

A Remarkable Happening

Santa Claus, finishing turkey and pie,
Rose from the table and uttered a sigh,
And said with a wink at his little round wife:
"As a cook, Mrs. S., you're the crown of my life!"
Then brushing the crumbs of his banquet away,
He ran from the house and jumped into his sleigh.

Climbing a roof, Santa sat on its peak,
Sorting his gifts with his tongue in his cheek.
Then smiling, he waved at the slumbering town,
And climbing a chimney, he let himself down.
But suddenly, dear, his expression of buoyance
Changed to a look of astonished annoyance!
His holiday dinner had made him so stout,
He couldn't get down—and he couldn't get out!
He wiggled and wriggled, but Santa, by Jim'ney,
Was stuck like a jolly red cork in the chimney!

"Help!" Santa cried with the wind in his beard.
Windowpanes opened, and nightcaps appeared.
People ran out, rather scantily shirted;
The Mayor was called, the police were alerted!
Children looked on with delighted hysterics
As firemen worked with their pulleys and derricks
Till finally Santa emerged with a flop,
Coming uncorked with an audible pop!

Well, somehow, my dears, he delivered his gifts,
Then homeward he flew over mountains and drifts;
And humbled, and puzzled, and risking her censure,
He told Mrs. Claus of his hapless adventure.
Patting his shoulder, she comforted him.
"Nonsense!" she said. "You are splendidly trim!
Come finish the pie—and don't worry or fear—
The chimneys are just getting smaller, my dear!"

Key Words

alert (ə lûrt) v. to warn; notify of approaching danger or action
Alerted by the weather bureau, Florida prepared for a hurricane.

annoyance (ə noi′əns) n. vexation; irritation
To my father's **annoyance**, our puppy chewed a hole in his golf bag.

audible (ô′də bəl) adj. capable of being heard
The voice on the phone was barely **audible**, so I said, "Would you please speak a little louder?"

banquet (băng′kwĭt) n. an elaborate dinner
The townspeople had a huge **banquet** to honor the new mayor.

buoyance (boi′yəns) n. cheerfulness; lightness of spirit
My friend never lost his **buoyance**, even when everything went wrong.

censure (sĕn′shər) n. blame or disapproval
The boy expected **censure** from his teacher because he was late again for his violin lesson.

crown (kroun) n. the highest or most perfect state or type; acme
Seeing the pyramids was the **crown** of my trip to Egypt.

derrick (dĕr′ĭk) n. a large crane for lifting objects
The **derrick** lifted the old cars and dropped them on the junk heap.

drift (drĭft) n. a pile of sand or snow, heaped up by the wind
After the blizzard, **drifts** of snow almost covered our windows.

emerge (ĭ mûrj) v. to rise up or come forth
A squirrel **emerged** from a hole high up in the tree and ran down the trunk.

Key Words

hapless (hăp′lĭs) adj. luckless; unfortunate
The first time she wore her new skates, the **hapless** girl tripped and sprained her ankle.

humble (hŭm′bəl) adj. having a feeling of insignificance; abashed
The champion tennis player was such a poor sport, the crowd hoped he would be **humbled** by a defeat.

hysterics (hĭ stĕr′ĭks) n. a fit of uncontrollable laughter
The children at the circus had **hysterics** when the clowns played basketball with the chimps.

pulley (pŏŏl′ē) n. a machine for lifting weight with a pulling force
The man used **pulleys** to haul the logs onto the truck.

risk (rĭsk) v. expose to a chance of loss or danger
My mother said I'd better wear a coat or I'd **risk** pneumonia.

scantily (skăn′tə lē) adv. barely sufficient or adequately
When the fire alarm rang in the hotel, **scantily** dressed people ran out of their rooms.

stout (stout) adj. bulky in figure; overweight
The woman was so **stout**, she had trouble getting out of the cab.

uncork (ŭn kôrk′) v. to free from a constrained state
When the roly-poly clown got stuck in the barrel, it took two of his friends to **uncork** him.

utter (ŭt′ər) v. to express audibly
When I woke from a terrible nightmare, I **uttered** a sigh of relief.

wriggle (rĭg′əl) v. to turn or twist the body with writhing motions; squirm
Unable to pay for tickets to the circus, the boys **wriggled** through a small opening under the tent.

Comprehension Check

Check the answer.

1. Santa Claus thought his wife was

   ____a. a good cook
   ____b. pleasingly plump
   ____c. a poor housekeeper

2. As he started down the chimney, Santa was annoyed to find

   ____a. a fire in the fireplace
   ____b. he was stuck
   ____c. he had forgotten the presents

3. Santa's holiday dinner had

   ____a. given him indigestion
   ____b. made him sleepy
   ____c. made him stouter

Fill in the blanks in the paragraph with the following words:

   emerged   delivered   wiggled and wriggled   had hysterics   ran out

   When Santa got stuck in the chimney he _____. Half dressed people
                                                            (4)
   _____of their houses. Delighted children _____. With the help of
        (5)   (6)
   firemen, Santa finally _____ and _____ the presents.
                                 (7)   (8)

9. Mrs. Santa could best be described as

   ____a. tactful and loving
   ____b. critical and bossy
   ____c. proud of her cooking

10. This story is mainly about

   ____a. how Santa got stuck in the chimney
   ____b. how firemen use pulleys and derricks
   ____c. why children are delighted with Santa

Think about: What is the most embarrassing thing that ever happened to you?

_____

_____

_____

The Remedy

A certain king of great renown
Saw everybody upside down.
It much disturbed him day and night,
So topsy-turvy was his sight.

To try to cure the good king's eyes
There came a doctor old and wise
Who dosed the king with horrid brews,
And poured red pepper in his shoes.

These things the patient king endured,
But when the doctor cried, "You're cured!"
His Highness blinked and glumly said:
"Sir! **Must** you stand upon your head?"

Came other clever doctors, then,
Distinguished and important men.
"The Cold Cure is the very thing!"
Said they, "Let's try it on the king!"

They promptly wrapped him in a sheet
With lumps of ice at head and feet.
Although it was a famous one,
This cure was very little fun.

"You're healed!" they cried. "Without a doubt,
Your sickness has been frozen out!"
But they were wrong—for all that froze
Was just the royal nose and toes.

Well, being men of great resource,
They tried the Hot Cure next, of course.
But though they baked him toe to brow,
His sole response to this was "OW!"

Then came a wizard, tall of hat,
Who cured the king as quick as **that**!
He simply turned him upside down
And stood His Highness on his crown.

"Hooray!" The king's relief was vast.
"You all look right side up, at last!"

Key Words

brew (broo) n. a drink made by boiling or mixing various ingredients
The old lady's favorite **brew** was hot mulberry tea with a slice of lemon.

brow (brou) n. forehead
The mother felt her little girl's **brow** to see if she had a fever.

distinguished (dĭs tĭng′gwĭsht) adj. eminent; renowned
Many **distinguished** scientists were invited to the meeting at the White House.

disturb (dĭs tûrb′) v. to upset
I was **disturbed** to find that my mother had thrown out my collection of bottle caps.

dose (dōs) v. to give medicine
I told my mother I'd rather be sick than **dosed** with castor oil.

glumly (glŭm′lē) adv. dejectedly, gloomily
Jill looked **glumly** out the window as the rain poured down, spoiling the picnic.

Highness (hī′nĭs) n. a title of honor for royalty
The page bowed low to the king and said, "I have a letter for you, Your **Highness**."

remedy (rĕm′ə dē) n. something that corrects a disorder
Our mother's **remedy** for swear words was to wash our mouths out with soap.

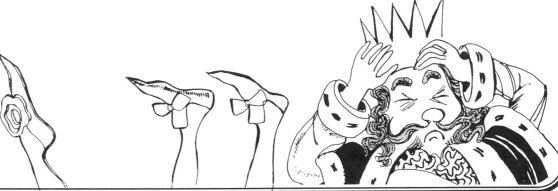

resource (rē sôrś) n. an ability to deal with a situation effectively
The mayor used great **resource** in dealing with the flood.

response (rĭ spŏnś) n. a reply or answer
His **response** to my question was so soft, I could hardly hear it.

sole (sōl) adj. single; only
My dad's **sole** excuse for breaking his promise was that he'd changed his mind.

topsy-turvy (tŏṕsē-tûŕvē) adv. upside down
Someone had opened my bureau drawers; all my clothes were **topsy-turvy**.

vast (văst) adj. very great
The boy and the old fisherman had become good friends, despite the **vast** difference in their ages.

wizard (wĭźərd) n. a sorcerer or magician
Some **wizards** are wiser and more powerful than others.

Comprehension Check

Check the answer.

1. The king had a problem with

    ____ a. blurry eyesight
    ____ b. seeing double
    ____ c. topsy-turvy eyesight

2. Hoping to cure the king, a wise old doctor

    ____ a. prescribed two aspirin before meals
    ____ b. poured red pepper in his shoes
    ____ c. told him he needed more sleep

3. The king could best be described as

    ____ a. patient
    ____ b. arrogant
    ____ c. cowardly

Fill in the blanks in the paragraph with the following words:

   the Cold Cure   head and feet   toe to brow   their remedies   the Hot Cure

   Other clever doctors tried _____. They wrapped the king's _____
                                                (4)   (5)
   with ice, but when _____ didn't work, they tried _____. Baking
                                        (6)   (7)
   the king from _____ didn't help either.
                             (8)

9. A wizard cured the king by

    ____ a. standing him on his head
    ____ b. giving him artificial respiration
    ____ c. giving him a strong pair of glasses

10. This poem is mainly about

    ____ a. medicine men
    ____ b. a king's eyesight problem
    ____ c. famous cures

Think about: If you were a wizard, how would you use your power? Answer in verse, if you like.

_____

_____

The Mischievous Rocket

I was watching the Mayor who, genial and spry,
Was setting off rockets one Fourth of July,
When all of a sudden the crowd gave a shout
For the Mayor was leaping and running about!

I leaned from my seat as I saw that a rocket
Had happened to catch on the flap of his pocket.
Well, it sizzled and hissed for a moment or two,
And then it went up—**and the Mayor went, too**!

High over rooftops and valleys and parks,
Up he went rapidly, shooting off sparks.
Then the rocket said "Boom!" in a rollicking voice,
And the Mayor came down. (He had no other choice.)

His hat flew away and his coattails unraveled
As straight for the earth he unwillingly traveled.
Then, ending his trip with a good deal of dash,
He fell in a lake with a spirited splash.
Emerging, he looked rather funny, I vow,
With a little green frog decorating his brow.

Since then, I admit I am likely to scoff
At well-behaved rockets that merely go off,
For **I** like a rocket that's daring and gay—
Like the one that went off with the Mayor that day!

Key Words

brow (brou) n. the forehead
His **brow** was deeply lined because of his constant frowning.

coattail (kōt′tāl) n. the back part of a coat below the waist
His **coattails** caught in the revolving door.

decorate (dĕk′ə rāt) v. to add something to make more attractive; adorn
The family always **decorated** the tree one week before Christmas.

emerge (ĭ murj′) v. to come forth into view, to become visible
The shivering swimmers **emerged** from the icy sea.

genial (jēn′yəl) adj. kindly; cheerful
Tommy's **genial** uncle bought him popcorn and a balloon.

hiss (hĭs) v. to make a sibilant hissing sound
"Sit down!" **hissed** the woman behind me. "I can't see the movie!"

mayor (mā′ər) n. chief executive of a city
The **mayor** was reelected to office for the fourth time.

merely (mîr′lē) adv. no more than; only
Although she was **merely** a child, she knew she wanted to be a doctor.

mischievous (mĭs′chə vəs) adj. prankish; full of tricks
The **mischievous** child was scolded by her parents for teasing the cat.

rapidly (răp′ĭd lē) adv. with great speed; swiftly
As the hill became steeper, my sled began to move more **rapidly**.

rollicking (rŏl′ĭ kĭng) adj. romping; high-spirited
Laughing and **rollicking**, the children played Last Tag until the sun went down

scoff (skŏf) v. to mock at or deride
The man **scoffed** when the doctor told him he should give up smoking.

sizzle (sĭz′əl) v. to make a hissing sound when in contact with heat
The pancakes **sizzled** on the hot grill.

spirited (spĭr′ĭ tĭd) adj. full of vigor; animated
As we left the stable, I hoped I could control my **spirited** horse.

spry (sprī) adj. full of life; active; nimble
The **spry** old man was still able to beat his son at tennis.

unravel (ŭn răv′əl) v. to undo; to separate something woven or tangled
The baby had found her mother's knitting and was **unraveling** it.

Comprehension Check

Check the answer.

1. The Mayor was celebrating

 ____ a. St. Patrick's Day
 ____ b. the Fourth of July
 ____ c. his birthday

2. What got caught in the Mayor's pocket?

 ____ a. a pickpocket's hand
 ____ b. his wallet
 ____ c. a rocket

3. The rocket caused the Mayor to be

 ____ a. shot into the air
 ____ b. blown to bits
 ____ c. covered with soot

Fill in the blanks in the paragraph with the following words:

rocket   splash   leaping and running about   pocket   genial and spry   lake

The Mayor was _____. He started _____ because a
                         (4)   (5)
_____ got caught in his _____. The Mayor landed with a _____ in
          (6)   (7)   (8)
a _____.
              (9)

10. This poem is mainly about

 ____ a. fun on the Fourth of July
 ____ b. how to have a celebration
 ____ c. the Mayor's rocket trip

Think about: How would you set off rockets in complete safety?

_____

_____

_____

_____

_____

_____

_____

The Shepherd and the Wolf

A shepherd boy, Horatius Hull,
Found tending sheep a trifle dull.
He could have studied botany
To help relieve monotony.
Instead, to give the town a fright,
He cried, "Wolf, wolf!" with all his might.
The townsfolk, seizing stick and rock,
Ran up, of course, to save his flock.
"Ha, ha!" came Hull's delighted shout;
"I fooled you! There's no wolf about!"

Next day, a wolf with drooling fang
Espied a sheep. He crouched and sprang.
"Mercy me!" and "Goodness gracious!"
Cried the much dismayed Horatius.
"Help! Wolf, wolf! Come quick, come quick!"
But none rushed up with stone or stick.
He'd tricked the town, the foolish dunce,
But he could only do it, **once**!
A liar's not believed, forsooth,
Even when he tells the truth.

Key Words

botany (bŏt′n ē) n. the biological science of plants
She had always been interested in plant life, so **botany** was her favorite subject.

crouch (krouch) v. to stoop with the limbs close to the body
The hunter saw a panther **crouched** on the limb of a tree.

dismay (dĭs mā′) v. to trouble greatly; make anxious or afraid
I was **dismayed** when I saw how poorly I had done on the test.

drool (drōōl) v. to let saliva run from the mouth
My dog began to **drool** when he saw Dad put the steaks on the grill.

dull (dŭl) adj. tedious
Bill enjoyed the town meeting; it wasn't as **dull** as he thought it would be.

dunce (dŭns) n. a stupid person; numbskull
He felt like a **dunce** when he couldn't solve the puzzle as quickly as his friend.

espy (ĕs pī′) v. to catch sight of
On the top of the cliff, she **espied** an eagle's nest.

fang (făng) n. a long, pointed tooth
When the boy tried to approach the young wildcat, it snarled and bared its **fangs**.

forsooth (fôr sooth') adv. in truth; indeed
As Shakespeare might say: "All's well that end's well, **forsooth**!"

monotony (mə nŏt'n ē) n. wearisome sameness
The night watchman didn't mind the **monotony** of his job as long as he had a good book.

relieve (rĭ lēv') v. to remove the monotony of; ease
My boredom was **relieved** when I saw two of my friends at the party.

shepherd (shĕp'ərd) n. one who herds and cares for sheep
A **shepherd** must stay awake in order to watch for wolves and other wild animals.

townsfolk (tounz'fōk) n. the inhabitants of a town
The **townsfolk** hoped to raise enough money to build a new school.

trifle (trī'fəl) adv. somewhat; a little
The sleeves were a **trifle** long, but the tailor said he would shorten them.

Comprehension Check

Check the answer.

1. Horatius thought tending sheep was

   ____a. an important responsibility
   ____b. boring and monotonous
   ____c. a good job

2. To stir up some excitement, Horatius

   ____a. let some sheep escape
   ____b. teased some sheep with sticks and stones
   ____c. cried wolf

3. The townsfolk helped Horatius by

   ____a. running up the mountain with sticks and stones
   ____b. finding the lost sheep
   ____c. killing the wolf

Fill in the blanks in the paragraph with the following words:

   wolf   rescue   believe   townsfolk   lie

Horatius fooled the _____ by pretending there was a _____. When a
                          (4)   (5)
real wolf suddenly appeared, the townsfolk didn't _____ Horatius. Horatius
                                                          (6)
was foolish to _____ because no one came to his _____ when he truly
                     (7)   (8)
needed help.

9. Being truthful is important because

   ____a. liars are not believed even when they tell the truth
   ____b. it is embarrassing to be caught in a lie
   ____c. liars don't have many friends

10. This poem is mainly about

   ____a. a shepherd who was bored
   ____b. a shepherd whose lying got him into trouble
   ____c. how to tend sheep

Think about: Can you think of a time when you or someone you know played games with the
truth? Explain the circumstances. What were the consequences?

Solomon's Travels

Solomon Solomon lived in a house
   Whose little red roof had a leak;
Its dusty old shutters were gusty with mutters,
   Its gate had a shivery squeak.

No stranger or friend ever entered his door,
   Which suited old Solomon, quite;
Alone (but not lonely) he did one thing only
   He read to himself day and night.

One evening, it chanced as he sat in his bed,
   Propped up in his quilts with a tale,
A rumble and mumble and ominous grumble
   Announced an incredible gale!

It loosened the shutters, it toppled the gate,
   It hoisted the trees from the lawn!
It swooped like a giant, rip-roaring, defiant,
   And scattered things hither and yon!

But Solomon Solomon chuckled and crowed
   And read to himself with delight,
So he failed to perceive when his chimney took leave
   And his roof sailed away like a kite!

Nor did he observe when the wind picked him up
   Where he rested so cozy and warm,
And blew him, unheeding (still placidly reading!),
   Aloft on the wings of the storm!

Above his abode the good gentleman rode
    Unconscious of tremors and jars;
In nightcap and tassel, past cottage and castle,
    He happily headed for Mars!

The crows were excited, the blue jays affrighted,
    As Solomon (reading) flew by;
And the eagles and hawks with imperious squawks
    Disputed his right to the sky!

The Milky Way curdled as over he hurdled!
    Astronomers, finding his range,
In awe and surprise opened scholarly eyes
    At the sight of a comet so strange!

But just about day, when the wind died away,
    He started a sudden descent!
Without worry or care he tobogganed the air,
    Turning a page as he went.

Yes, head over heels Mr. Solomon fell,
    And contrary heels over head,
Until with a flip he concluded his trip,
    Somersaulting right back into bed!

Then yawning and stretching, he murmured:"Ho-hum!
    What a stay-at-home body I be!"
And closing his book with a faraway look,
    "I wish I could travel!" said he.

Key Words

abode (ə bōd) n. home; a place where one lives or stays
Their **abode** was on a hill, nestled among trees.

affright (ə frīt) v. to frighten; alarm
The little girl was **affrighted** by the Halloween witches.

astronomer (ə strŏn′ə mər) n. a scientist specializing in astronomy
The **astronomers** predicted correctly the time when the comet could be seen.

conclude (kən klōōd) v. to bring to a close; finish
He **concluded** the written assignment at 11:30 p.m.

contrary (kŏn′trĕr ē) adj. opposite in nature; altogether different
His idea of a good vacation was **contrary** to mine—he wanted to play golf, and I wanted to go on a cruise.

crow (krō) v. to make a sound expressive of pleasure; to exult
How my friend **crowed** when he won his bet!

curdle (kûrd′l) v. to congeal; to form into a curd; to horrify
The monster's screams **curdled** my blood.

defiant (dĭ fī′ənt) adj. bold; insolent
The **defiant** workers refused to return to their jobs.

dispute (dĭs pyōōt) v. to argue; debate
Mr. Jones **disputed** his neighbor's right to raise chickens in his backyard.

hither (hĭth′ər) adv. to this place; here
"Come **hither**," said the spider to the fly.

hoist (hoist) v. to raise aloft; pull up
The sailors **hoisted** the anchor from the sea.

ominous (ŏm′ə nəs) adj. threatening; sinister
The **ominous** dark clouds warned us that a thunderstorm was coming.

perceive (pər sēv′) v. to take note of; comprehend
Most of the readers **perceived** the true meaning of the poem.

placidly (plăs′ĭd lē) adv. calmly; tranquilly
Her brothers were having a noisy fight, but the little girl **placidly** went on reading her book.

prop (prŏp) v. to support; hold up
The mother **propped** the baby's back with a pillow.

swoop (swoōp) v. to descend suddenly; pounce upon
The eagle **swooped** down on a flock of sparrows.

toboggan (tə bŏg′ən) v. to coast; ride a toboggan
The children spent all afternoon **tobogganing** down the hill.

topple (tŏp′əl) v. to push over; overturn
In his hurry to escape, the thief had **toppled** a statue in the hallway.

unheeding (ŭn hēd′ĭng) adj. careless; unmindful
Many accidents are caused by **unheeding** drivers.

Comprehension Check

Check the answer.

1. Solomon enjoyed

    ____a. working in his garden
    ____b. reading
    ____c. painting pictures

2. One night when Solomon was in bed

    ____a. the bed broke
    ____b. lightning struck the house
    ____c. the wind blew the roof off his house

3. While flying through the air, Solomon was

    ____a. frightened and screaming
    ____b. still reading
    ____c. asleep in his bed

Fill in the blanks in the paragraph with the following words:

      astronomers   comet   somersaulted   fell   blue jays and crows

When Solomon flew through the air, the _____ were excited. _____
(4)   (5)

thought they were seeing a _____. Solomon _____ head over heels,
(6)   (7)

then _____ back into bed.
(8)

9. Solomon could best be described as

    ____a. nervous and excitable
    ____b. a fair-weather friend
    ____c. calm and unruffled

10. This poem is mainly about

    ____a. fun and fantasy
    ____b. the joy of reading
    ____c. how to travel by air
    ____d. a bookworm

Think about: How would you travel to a faraway place? Plan the trip.

_____

_____

_____

The Stranger

As I was walking through a wood, one cool September day,
I chanced to see a stranger standing jaunty, in my way.
There wasn't much about him to remark about, I guess—
Unless it might be possibly the matter of his dress.
I couldn't help from noticing the jacket he had on,
For glory be! 'Twas greener than McGillicuddy's lawn!
Except for that, there wasn't much to stretch a pair of eyes—
Unless I should be mentioning the matter of his size!
It's really rather seldom you'll be meeting, on your walks,
A bit of man who measures seven inches in his socks.

I looked at him and **looked** at him and kinda thought it over,
While he stared back, his little head just level with the clover.
"You're not a native of the town!" I presently decided.
"No, that I'm not!" the little man quite cheerfully confided.
"Well then," I went on thoughtful-like, as sharp I looked him through,
"I'm thinking you're a stranger, here." Said he: "I think so, too!"
Said I: "Could be that you're a man who's kinda **shrunk** a little!"
"It could be now!" he answered me, a trifle noncommittal.
Then, standing up all fine and straight, he faced me like a hero.
(The brash of him whose size was little more than two times zero!)
Then sweeping off his tiny cap, he said with quite a bow:
"Good luck to you, long life to you—and I'll be leaving, now!"

With that, the little fellow went. 'Twas queer, I do declare!
He didn't walk away from me. He simply **wasn't there**!

Well, as I wandered homeward with the sunlight in my eyes,
I talked it over with myself. (Myself is wondrous wise!)
Said I: "He was a pipe dream! Aye! He surely was the type!"
"Fiddlesticks!" Myself replied. "You've never owned a pipe."

And thinkin' of the matter, very sober in the dawn,
The both of us decided I had met a leprechaun!

Key Words

confide (kən fīd′) v. to tell something privately
Anne **confided** to her sister that she liked the boy next door.

fiddlesticks (fĭd′l stĭks′) interj. expression of annoyance or impatience
"Fiddlesticks!" said Mom. "It's raining out, and I didn't bring an umbrella!"

homeward (hōm′wərd) adv. toward home
We stopped to get books at the library and then began walking **homeward**.

jaunty (jôn′tē) adj. self-confident; carefree
My little brother was so pleased with his new baseball cap that he wore it with a **jaunty** air all day long.

level (lĕv′əl) adj. being at the same height as another; even
Tom's head was **level** with the basketball net, so it was easy for him to make baskets.

mention (mĕn′shən) v. to refer briefly to something
When I **mentioned** my older brother's name, my history teacher remembered him well.

noncommittal (nŏn′kə mĭt′l) adj. reticent; refraining from taking a stand
I didn't want to take sides in the argument, so I remained **noncommittal**.

pipe dream (pīp′drēm′) n. a fantastic notion or hope
Her friends thought her wish to be a champion skater was just a **pipe dream**.

shrink (shrĭngk) v. to contract; become reduced in size
My wool sweater had **shrunk** because my mother put it in the washing machine by mistake.

stretch (strĕch) v. to widen or lengthen or both
He was so happy, his grin **stretched** from ear to ear.

wondrous (wŭn′drəs) adj. wonderful
At the end of the day, there was a **wondrous** display of fireworks in the park.

This is your space. You may:
    a. draw a picture about the poem
    b. write a story
    c. write a poem
    d. write a paragraph
Use at least three key words for b, c, or d.

Comprehension Check

Check the answer.

1. The stranger was dressed in

   ____ a. a yellow jacket
   ____ b. a clown suit
   ____ c. a green jacket

2. The stranger was

   ____ a. short and fat
   ____ b. six feet tall
   ____ c. seven inches tall

3. Where did the stranger go?

   ____ a. to Washington, D.C.
   ____ b. into thin air
   ____ c. to his psychiatrist

Fill in the blanks in the paragraph with the following words:

   cap   pipe dream   woods   jacket

   The stranger was first seen in the _____. The stranger was wearing a green
                                            (4)
   _____ and a tiny _____. Was this happening a _____?
          (5)   (6)   (7)

8-9. The stranger could best be described as (check two)

   ____ a. a tiny person
   ____ b. a ghost
   ____ c. a leprechaun
   ____ d. a hunter

10. This poem is mainly about

   ____ a. an afternoon in the woods
   ____ b. a meeting with a leprechaun
   ____ c. friends and strangers
   ____ d. pipe dreams

Think about: What would you do if you came upon a leprechaun? Answer in verse, if you like.

_____

_____

_____

Ulysses and the Cyclops

This particular tale I'm preparing to tell
Will chill you, my hearties, I tell it so well!
So pull on your sweaters is now my advice,
Or the story that follows will turn you to ice.
(And that wouldn't be nice.)

Ulysses had taken a long ocean-trip.
He was weary of sailing so, beaching his ship,
He and his mariners, bearded and brave,
Took refuge, one day, in a gloomy old cave.
"Does anyone live here?" Ulysses cried out.
"I DO!" came a raucous, ear-deafening shout . . . .
And there, at the door of the cavernous hall
Stood a Cyclops, one-eyed and eleven feet tall!
He stared at Ulysses. "Who **are** you?" he cried;
"I'm Noman!" quick-witted Ulysses replied.
The Cyclops then lowered his single-eyed stare
On the mariners, standing uneasily there.
"Welcome, my friends!" cried this jovial sinner,
"You're just in good time, as it happens, for dinner!"
This sounded quite friendly and kind in intent,
But the mariners paled, for they knew what he meant!

By the time that the Cyclops had finished his feast
The mariners' number had greatly decreased.
At Ulysses (left over) he hungrily stared.
"I'll eat you tomorrow!" the Cyclops declared.
Now, Ulysses who stood where the shadows were thick,
Had been slyly and secretly whittling a stick.
This dangerous dagger he up and let fly . . .
And it struck the old Cyclops kerplunk in the eye.
(This is the kind of adventure, my hearties,
The Greeks used to tell at polite little parties!)

The Cyclops let out such a harrowing yelp
That his great clumsy brothers came running to help.
"Who hurt you?" they asked the unfortunate fellow;
"Noman!" he cried at the top of his bellow.
"Well, brother," they stated with vehement virtue,
"You don't need assistance if no man has hurt you!"
As the giants departed, Ulysses ran out—
To have more adventures, I haven't a doubt.

This is the ancient account of Ulysses,
A story which wasn't intended for sissies!

Key Words

account (ə kount′) n. description; narrative
We all wanted to hear Tom's **account** of what happened during the flood.

beach (bēch) v. to haul or run onto a beach
Nearing the shore, he **beached** his rowboat and ran toward his friend's house.

bellow (bĕl′ō) n. roar
The steer gave a **bellow** when he was branded.

cavernous (kăv′ər nəs) adj. hollow; like a cave
The secret stairway led to a huge, **cavernous** room.

chill (chĭl) v. to make chilly or shivery
John was **chilled** when he heard that the tornado had struck homes in his neighborhood.

declare (dĭ klār′) v. to proclaim; state
The umpire **declared** that the game was a tie.

decrease (dĭ krēs′) v. to diminish; become smaller in number
At the end of September, the boats in the harbor began to **decrease**.

harrowing (har′ō ĭng) adj. painfully distressing
The parents spent a **harrowing** and sleepless night, wondering where their son was.

intent (ĭn tĕnt′) n. purpose; intention
It was my **intent** to get up at dawn, but I slept through the alarm.

jovial (jō′vē əl) adj. jolly; having a joyous humor
Our **jovial** Uncle Fred used to tell us funny stories about his boyhood.

kerplunk (kər plŭngk′) adv. with a muffled thud
The puppy slipped on the ice and landed **kerplunk** in a snowbank.

mariner (mâr′ə nər) n. seaman; sailor
After six months at sea, the **mariners** were glad to see their home port.

pale (pāl) v. to lose color; turn white
When the pilot invited me for a ride, I **paled** and said I would think about it.

particular (pər tĭk′yə lər) adj. special; especial
This **particular** book was given to me by my grandmother.

prepare (prĭ pâr′) v. to get ready
She's **preparing** to leave for a vacation in Switzerland.

quick-witted (kwĭk′ wĭt ĭd) adj. having a nimble, alert mind
Finding the telephone dead, the **quick-witted** girl used her CB radio to call for help.

raucous (rô′kəs) adj. harsh; grating
Uncle Harry had a **raucous** laugh and liked to smoke big cigars.

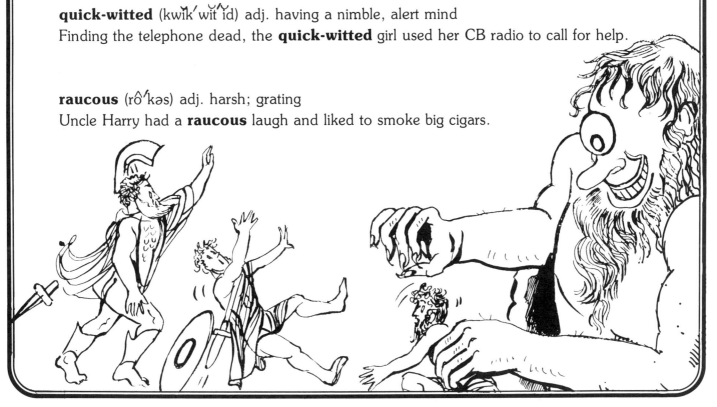

sinner (sĭn′ər) n. transgressor; one who breaks a moral or religious law
A person can go to church every Sunday and still be a **sinner**.

uneasily (ŭn ē zə lē) adv. uncomfortably; restlessly
She left for school **uneasily**, feeling that she had forgotten something.

vehement (vē′ə mənt) adj. ardent; intense
The old man showed **vehement** dislike of any helpful advice.

virtue (vûr′chōō) n. righteousness; goodness
His patience with his children was one of his many **virtues**.

weary (wîr′ē) adj. tired
She was so **weary**, she fell asleep in the middle of the movie.

whittle (hwĭt′l) v. to shape a piece of wood with a knife
The old sailor spent many hours **whittling** birds and animals from pieces of driftwood.

Comprehension Check

Check the answer.

1. Ulysses beached his ship because

____a. it had a big hole in the hull
____b. he needed more food
____c. he was tired of sailing

2. The Cyclops was

____a. a real person
____b. a one-eyed giant
____c. a dragon

Check the answer that is **not** true.

3. The Cyclops was glad to see the mariners because

____a. he needed food for dinner
____b. he thought they'd make a tasty meal
____c. he was lonely

Fill in the blanks in the paragraph with the following words:

   "Noman"   dinner   main course   the giants

The Cyclops invited the mariners to _____. The mariners were unhappy be-
                 (4)
cause they knew they were the _____. Ulysses saved himself by saying he was
             (5)
_____. When _____ left, Ulysses was able to escape.
 (6)   (7)

Check two.

8-9. How did Ulysses save himself?
____a. He called the police.
____b. The mariners rescued him.
____c. He whittled a dagger and wounded the Cyclops.
____d. He called himself "Noman."

10. This poem is mainly about

____a. Greek parties
____b. a friendly banquet
____c. Cyclops and his brothers
____d. a one-eyed giant and Ulysses

Think about: What would you do if a modern Cyclops appeared at your door? Answer in verse,
     if you like.

Terminology Check

Study the glossary (page 116); then, from the following list, choose the terms which best describe the phrases listed below.

alliteration   personification
hyperbole   pun
internal rhyme   sibilance
metaphor   simile
onomatopoeia

1. one speck had stopped Bert in his track   _____

2. gurgle-and-slosh day   _____

3. Yelchior, dressed in his black and his white   _____

4. a donkey roly-poly, ambling lazily and slowly   _____

5. frolicked around like a lovable pup   _____

6. much to the pleasure and profit of Pat   _____

7. arriving at a river which he waded with a shiver   _____

8. the ocean's cello   _____

9. your hunger let greediness open the throttle   _____

10. you'll learn as you travel the years   _____

11. Poor fish! With sad emotion he envied all his scornful kin   _____

12. he was, you might say, "oystracized"   _____

13. all fin-land knew   _____

14. he'd leap and prance or jog or dance   _____

15. was stuck like a jolly red cork in the chimney   _____

16. sizzled and hissed (two possible answers)   _____

17. his roof sailed away like a kite   _____

18. crows were excited, blue jays affrighted   _____

19. the story that follows will turn you to ice   _____

20. single-eyed stare   _____

Vocabulary Check

Check the correct definition for each word in bold. You may find the answers more quickly if you check to see what part of speech is involved. For example, the word *light* has various meanings, depending on whether it is a noun (illumination), a verb (to ignite), or an adjective (weightless). The word *cross* can mean irritable (adjective), hardship (noun), or to transverse (verb).

1. **grubby** - adj.
____a. buggy
____b. dirty
____c. gray

2. **malevolent** - adj.
____a. kindly
____b. violent
____c. malicious

3. **amble** - v.
____a. to walk slowly
____b. to browse
____c. to roam

4. **stoke** - v.
____a. to sulk
____b. to tend a stove
____c. to stow away

5. **crafty** - adj.
____a. skillful
____b. nimble
____c. shrewd

6. **wager** - v.
____a. to bet
____b. to earn
____c. to assume

7. **vexed** - adj.
____a. annoyed
____b. depressed
____c. bewitched

8. **ambition** - n.
____a. greed
____b. zeal
____c. energy

9. **moderation** - n.
____a. renovation
____b. dignity
____c. restraint

10. **bluster** - v.
____a. to strike
____b. to bully
____c. to disagree

11. **ostracize** - v.
____a. to exclude
____b. to honor
____c. to procrastinate

12. **remorse** - n.
____a. resentment
____b. regret
____c. uneasiness

13. **leisure** - n.
____a. hobby
____b. inaction
____c. spare time

14. **hapless** - adj.
____a. unfortunate
____b. accidental
____c. unhappy

15. **distinguished** - adj.
____a. solemn
____b. eminent
____c. vivacious

16. **rollicking** - adj.
____a tumbling
____b. high-spirited
____c. eager

17. **monotony** - n.
____a. isolation
____b. indifference
____c. boring sameness

18. **imperious** - adj.
____a. arrogant
____b. impudent
____c. important

19. **espy** - v.
____a. to spy on
____b. to catch sight of
____c. to escape

20. **harrowing** - adj.
____a. painfully distressing
____b. violently destructive
____c. careworn

21. **unspeakable** - adj.
____a. uncommunicative
____b. inexpressible
____c. stuttering

22. **emit** - v.
____a. to utter
____b. to allow
____c. to reject

23. **humdinger** - n.
____a. melody
____b. surprise
____c. marvel

24. **blithely** - adv.
____a. cheerfully
____b. delightfully
____c. contentedly

25. **smirk** - n.
_____a. chuckle
_____b. simper
_____c. jest

26. **scan** - v.
_____a. to examine
_____b. to hasten
_____c. to outwit

27. **glumly** - adv.
_____a. sullenly
_____b. resentfully
_____c. dejectedly

28. **captivating** - adj.
_____a. confined
_____b. fascinating
_____c. cavorting

29. **moral** - n.
_____a. lesson
_____b. painting
_____c. lecture

30. **tactful** - adj.
_____a. sharp
_____b. considerate
_____c. gentle

31. **solitude** - n.
_____a. loneliness
_____b. peace
_____c. aloneness

32. **respect** - n.
_____a. esteem
_____b. affection
_____c. concern

33. **renown** - n.
_____a. gossip
_____b. fame
_____c. rumor

34. **emerge** - v.
_____a. to join
_____b. to enter
_____c. to come forth

35. **vast** - adj.
_____a. stout
_____b. universal
_____c. very great

36. **genial** - adj.
_____a. cheerful
_____b. healthy
_____c. generous

37. **relieve** - v.
_____a. to relent
_____b. to rescue
_____c. to ease

38. **ominous** - adj.
_____a. unlucky
_____b. gloomy
_____c. threatening

39. **vehement** - adj.
_____a. angry
_____b. intense
_____c. resentful

40. **mellow** - v.
_____a. to mature
_____b. to polish
_____c. to tenderize

41. **assert** - v.
_____a. to declare
_____b. to agree
_____c. to argue

42. **fervor** - n.
_____a. heat
_____b. dismay
_____c. ardor

43. **bleary** - adj.
_____a. moody
_____b. blurred
_____c. hard of hearing

44. **imposing** - adj.
_____a. conceited
_____b. impressive
_____c. bold

45. **ponder** - v.
_____a. to consider
_____b. to remember
_____c. to daydream

46. **tweak** - v.
_____a. to twist
_____b. to tie
_____c. to yelp

47. **badger** - v.
_____a. to blame
_____b. to disturb
_____c. to pester

48. **shoddy** - adj.
_____a. ragged
_____b. inferior
_____c. shameful

49. **forlorn** - adj.
_____a. pitiful
_____b. lonesome
_____c. gloomy

50. **console** - v.
_____a. to help
_____b. to advise
_____c. to comfort

Use the ideas in the following work sheets as models and expand on them with your own innovations.

Fill in the blanks in the poem with the following words:

birds   stones   moans   words   today   whir   purr   stray

This poem uses end rhymes.

Silence Speaks

Kettles whistle, rockets _____,
(1)

Puppies bark and kittens _____,
(2)

Chimneys utter mournful _____,
(3)

Rivers chuckle over _____
(4)

But Silence **whispers**, using _____
(5)

And brooks and bumblebees for _____.
(6)

In the meadow where I _____
(7)

I heard Silence speak _____.
(8)

9. "Mutter mournful moans" is an example of

   ____a. assonance
   ____b. alliteration
   ____c. a simile

10. "I heard Silence speak" is an example of

   ____a. personification
   ____b. onomatopoeia
   ____c. a simile

The verses in the exercises on pages 109 and 110 are by Ernestine Cobern Beyer.

Fill in the blanks in the poem with the following words:

absurd   trees   breeze   bird   frog   please   heard   agog

This poem uses internal rhymes.

Happy Language

There once was a _____ with a musical wheeze,
       (1)

"Swish, swish!" was all she could say;

And this, if you _____, for a breeze in the _____,
       (2)   (3)

Means: "Oh! What a beautiful day!"

There once was a _____ all _____ in a bog,
       (4)   (5)

"Karrrump!" he would cry in delight;

And this, for a frog on a log in a bog,

Means: "Oh! What a beautiful night!"

There once was a _____, rather small and _____,
       (6)   (7)

"Tweet-tweet!" he would twitter and sing;

And this, I have _____, is a word for a bird
       (8)

Meaning: "OH! WHAT A WONDERFUL SPRING!"

9. "Karrrump!" is an example of

    _____a. onomatopoeia

    _____b. personification

    _____c. a metaphor

10. "And this, for a frog on a log in a bog" is an example of

    _____a. hyperbole

    _____b. an internal rhyme

    _____c. personification

A haiku is a poem which expresses a single thought or emotion in three lines (5/7/5 syllables) and usually concerns nature. Study the four examples below. The first three are translations of Japanese haiku.

1

In the city fields,
Contemplating cherry trees . . .
Strangers are like friends.

Issa

2

See the red berries . . .
Fallen like little foot prints
In the garden snow.

Shiki

3

Bony brushwood twigs
Cut down and stacked in bunches . . .
Yet bravely budding.

Boncho

4

A bitter morning:
Sparrows sitting together
Without any necks.

J. W. Hackett*

* (From Japan Airlines Haiku Contest, 1964)

Check the answer.

1. The first two haiku contain a figure of speech called

     ____a. personification
     ✓ b. a simile
     ____c. a metaphor

2. The first line of the haiku by Issa has

     ✓ a. five syllables
     ____b. four syllables
     ____c. seven syllables

3. In the haiku by Issa, strangers are like friends because

     ____a. strangers are trusted by Japanese people
     ____b. they bow and smile in a friendly way
     ✓ c. they are sharing a pleasant experience

4. In the haiku about brushwood twigs, Boncho uses

     ____a. internal rhymes
     ✓ b. alliteration
     ____c. sibilance

Check three.

5-7. These four haiku all have

     ____a. end rhymes
     ✓ b. 5/7/5 syllables
     ____c. onomatopoeia
     ✓ d. a single thought or emotion
     ✓ e. a connection with nature
     ____f. meter

Check the answer.

8. The middle line of the fourth haiku has

     ____a. three syllables
     ✓ b. seven syllables
     ____c. five syllables

9. In the fourth haiku, the weather is

     ____a. rainy
     ____b. springlike
     ✓ c. cold

10. The sparrows appear to have no necks because

     ____a. they are baby birds
     ✓ b. they are hunched up, trying to get warm
     ____c. they have had a big breakfast

Think about: The first haiku concerns city strangers becoming friends when sharing a pleasant experience. Tell about a time when you had a similar experience.

If you keep your senses alert, you will find ideas for haiku every day—even on your television! The lines below are quoted almost word for word from a nature program which contrasted the clumsiness of a hippopotamus on land with its grace in the water.

Hip po pot a mus es (or hip po pot a mi)	6 (or 5)
Tip toe a long the bot tom	7
Of the ri ver bed.	5

With a few slight changes, this haiku is created:

The hip po tip toes	5
Oh, so soft ly, on the floor	7
Of the ri ver bed.	5

A member of your family could be the subject of a haiku. The thought which follows was inspired by an elderly woman who was showing her grandchildren an old photograph album.

Her gnarled hands show us	5
Snap shots of her young er self . . .	7
Gram? On a cam el?	5

Nature is full of haiku, waiting to be discovered by poets!
A simple weed like the dandelion makes a fine subject:

O dan de li on!	5
Your sun ny curls will soon be	7
Turn ing white as snow.	5

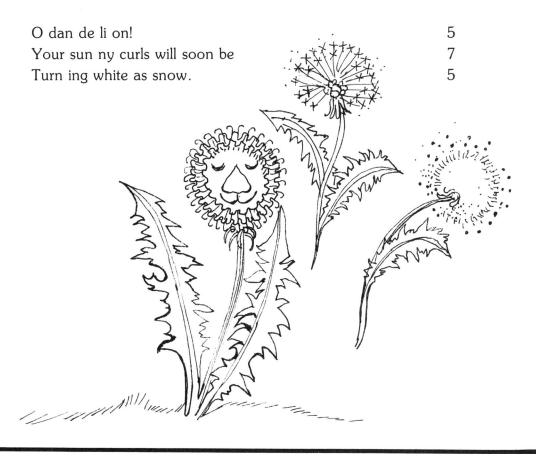

There are countless 5-syllable phrases which could be used for the first or last line of a haiku. Here are a few examples:

In the hush of dusk	Winter's frosty touch
Leaves are drifting down	The apple blossoms
The evening shadows	Indian summer
As the tide goes out	On the sandy shore
As the tide comes in	A newborn kitten
A blustering wind	My baby sister (or brother)
The cat, tail switching	Streets glisten with rain

Using "In the hush of dusk" as the first line, you could complete the haiku with something like this:

In the hush of dusk	5
A crick et's trem u lous chord	7
Ush ers in the night.	5

A variation on the same theme:

As twi light deep ens	5
Crick ets are tun ing their wings . . .	7
Con cert time is here!	5

In the following haiku, "As the tide comes in" is used as the last line:

Tire less ly we toil . . .	5
Then watch our cas tles crum ble	7
As the tide comes in.	5

Here you are given the first two lines of a haiku. Try completing it with a thought of your own.

As the tide goes out,	5
Min nows left in shal low pools	7
_____ _____ _____ _____ _____.	5

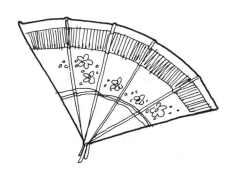

Try to **be** one of those minnows and imagine how you would feel. Would you miss your friends? Would the pool get too warm in the sun? Would you be an easy catch for cats and kids? Express what you feel in a 5-syllable line.

Now that you have been given a few ideas, we hope you find yourself eager to release the poet that is in you and all of us. Using the haiku form, try to capture a moment in nature in your own unique poem.

___ ___ ___ ___ ___ ___ ___ ___   5

___ ___ ___ ___ ___ ___ ___ ___ ___   7

___ ___ ___ ___ ___ ___ ___ .   5

Glossary

Alliteration: The repetition of initial sounds at the beginnings of two or more words

Assonance: The repetition of vowel sounds within words

Couplet: A pair of consecutive rhyming lines, usually having the same meter

Figurative Language: A picturesque use of words which makes the poet's meaning more vivid than a literal statement

Free Verse: Poetry without regularized meter, usually unrhymed

Haiku: A three-line poetic form (five/seven/five syllables), originally Japanese, and usually connected with nature

Hyperbole: An exaggeration or extravagant statement used as a figure of speech

Imagery: The written description of a mind-picture appealing to the reader's senses

Metaphor: An implied comparison between two generally unlike things, usually referring to one object, attribute, or action, as if it were another

Onomatopoeia: Words which imitate the sound they name such as **buzz**, **boom**, or **rumble**

Personification: A metaphor that attributes human characteristics to inanimate objects, animals, or abstract ideas

Pun: The use of two words that look or sound alike but have different meanings—often called a "play on words" (usually humorous)

Rhyme: Repetition of identical or similar sounds in unaccented syllables of words

>   **End Rhyme**: Rhyme occurring at the ends of lines
>
>   **Eye Rhyme**: Words which look alike but sound different (**rough** and **bough**)
>
>   **Internal Rhyme**: Rhyme occurring between words within a line or between words within different lines
>
>   **Rhyme Scheme**: The way in which a poet arranges rhymes

Rhythm: The recurrence of syllables at regular or expected intervals

Sibilance: Words which produce a hissing sound (sizzle, swish, whistle, sputter). Often onomatopoeic but characterized by the sound of **s**, **sh**, or **z**

Simile: A resemblance or comparison between two generally unlike things, usually introduced by "like" or "as"

Symbolism: A form of metaphor in which a person, place, thing, or quality stands for a more complex meaning

Answer Key

Page 5
Birthington's Washday
1. b.
2. c.
3. move
4. dirt
5. help
6. a hose
7. b.
8. d.
9. c.
10. c.

Page 10
The Concert
1. c.
2. b.
3. c.
4. cat
5. concert
6. thanks
7. shoes
8. awake
9. yowling
10. a.

Page 14
The Donkey and the Cricket
1. c.
2. c.
3. syrup
4. cricket
5. diet
6. dewdrops
7. moon
8. c.
9. a.
10. c.

Page 19
The Lovable Dragon
1. b.
2. c.
3. b.
4. children ran away from him
5. he looked so ferocious
6. orange and red smoke
7. his nostrils
8. corn
9. his head
10. a.

Page 25
The Emperor's Robe
1. b.
2. a.
3. b.
4. invisible
5. admit
6. thieves and rogues
7. pretend
8. b.
9. b.
10. b.

Page 26

Crossword solution:
- 1. BLUFF
- 4. TEE
- 6. GOWN / SPIN
- TREE
- SEE
- 13. ENCHANTED
- HAD
- 16. EEL / SNIP
- 18. UNDO

Page 30
The Honest Man
1. d.
2. c.
3. a scholar
4. an honest man
5. thieves
6. everywhere
7. reflection
8. d.
9. a.
10. b.

Page 35
The Magical Hat
1-2. b. d. f. g.
3. b.
4. c.
5. Halloween
6. a magical hat
7. a rabbit
8. people
9. c.
10. c.

Page 41
Meranda
1. b.
2. b.
3. enchanting
4. song
5. shell
6. sang
7. charmed
8. tune
9. c.
10. c.

Page 47
The Mouse and the Weasel
1. a.
2. b.
3. meals
4. host
5. barrel
6. corn
7-8. b. d.
9. d.
10. c.

Page 53
Essay on Mules
1. b.
2. c.
3. d.
4. sat down
5. prodded and pushed
6. stubborn
7. motivated
8-9. b. f.
10. b.

Page 59
The Oyster
1-3. a. c. e.
4. b.
5. c.
6. melancholy
7. uncomfortable
8. grievous
9. scornful
10. b.

Page 65
Peter the Puppet
1. b.
2. b.
3. c.
4. waltz
5. Fling
6. somersaults
7. vim
8. strings
9. b.
10. c.

Page 70
The Pied Piper of Hamelin
1. b.
2. c.
3. c.
4. sleepy
5. unbelievably sweet
6. fretful
7. merry
8. thankful
9. a.
10. c.

Page 75
A Remarkable Happening
1. a.
2. b.
3. c.
4. wiggled and wriggled
5. ran out
6. had hysterics
7. emerged
8. delivered
9. a.
10. a.

Page 81
The Remedy
1. c.
2. b.
3. a.
4. their remedies
5. head and feet
6. the Cold Cure
7. the Hot Cure
8. toe to brow
9. a.
10. b.

Page 85
The Mischievous Rocket
1. b.
2. c.
3. a.
4. genial and spry
5. leaping and running about
6. rocket
7. pocket
8. splash
9. lake
10. c.

Page 89
The Shepherd and the Wolf
1. b.
2. c.
3. a.
4. townsfolk
5. wolf
6. believe
7. lie
8. rescue
9. a.
10. b.

Page 94
Solomon's Travels
1. b.
2. c.
3. b.
4. blue jays and crows
5. Astronomers
6. comet
7. fell
8. somersaulted
9. c.
10. a.

Page 99
The Stranger
1. c.
2. c.
3. b.
4. woods
5. jacket
6. cap
7. pipe dream
8-9. a. c.
10. b.

Page 105
Ulysses and the Cyclops
1. c.
2. b.
3. c.
4. dinner
5. main course
6. "Noman"
7. the giants
8-9. c. d.
10. d.

Page 106
Terminology Check
1. hyperbole
2. onomatopoeia
3. personification
4. internal rhyme
5. simile
6. alliteration
7. internal rhyme
8. metaphor
9. metaphor
10. metaphor
11. personification
12. pun
13. pun
14. internal rhyme
15. simile
16. onomatopoeia; sibilance
17. simile
18. internal rhyme
19. metaphor
20. alliteration

Page 107
Vocabulary Check

1. b.	11. a.	21. b.	31. c.	41. a.
2. c.	12. b.	22. a.	32. a.	42. c.
3. a.	13. c.	23. c.	33. b.	43. b.
4. b.	14. a.	24. a.	34. c.	44. b.
5. c.	15. b.	25. b.	35. c.	45. a.
6. a.	16. b.	26. a.	36. a.	46. a.
7. a.	17. c.	27. c.	37. c.	47. c.
8. b.	18. a.	28. b.	38. c.	48. b.
9. c.	19. b.	29. a.	39. b.	49. a.
10. b.	20. a.	30. b.	40. a.	50. c.

Page 109
Silence Speaks
1. whir
2. purr
3. moans
4. stones
5. birds
6. words
7. stray
8. today
9. b.
10. a.

Page 110
Happy Language
1. breeze
2. please
3. trees
4. frog
5. agog
6. bird
7. absurd
8. heard
9. a.
10. b.

Page 112
Haiku
1. b.
2. a.
3. c.
4. b.
5-7. b. d. e.
8. b.
9. c.
10. b.